Team Players and Teamwork

JB JOSSEY-BASS

Team Players and Teamwork

New Strategies for Developing Successful Collaboration

Second Edition

Glenn M. Parker

John Wiley & Sons, Inc.

Published by Jossey-Bass
A Wiley Imprint
989 Market Street, San Francisco, CA 94103-1741—www.josseybass.com

Jossey-Bass books and products are available through most bookstores. To contact Jossey-Bass directly call our Customer Care Department within the U.S. at 800-956-7739, outside the U.S. at 317-572-3986, or fax 317-572-4002.

Jossey-Bass also publishes its books in a variety of electronic formats. Some content that appears in print may not be available in electronic books.

Library of Congress Cataloging-in-Publication Data

Parker, Glenn M.
    Team players and teamwork: new strategies for developing successful collaboration / Glenn M. Parker. –2nd ed.
        p. cm.
    Includes bibliographical references and index.
    ISBN-13: 978-0-7879-9811-0 (cloth)
        1. Teams in the workplace. 2. Corporate culture. I. Title.
HD66.P346 2008
658.4'022—dc22

Printed in the United States of America
SECOND EDITION
HB Printing   10 9 8 7 6 5 4 3 2 1

Contents

Preface

When *Team Players and Teamwork* was first published in 1990, we had already begun to see the emergence of teamwork as an important business strategy. The success of Japan as a world economic power in the 1960s and 1970s led to a fascination with Japanese management strategies and, in turn, to the popularity of quality circles, a team-based process improvement effort. Despite great success in a number of companies, quality circles failed to gain substantial support outside of manufacturing. Even when successful, quality circles were rarely part of an overall corporate strategy.

In the 1980s we saw the outline of an emerging movement toward self-directed teams, as well as a total quality management process that was heavily team-based. These "solutions" were followed by another series of fads, the most prominent of which was reengineering. Later we witnessed a fascination with something called a *high performing organization*. These approaches—reengineering and high performing organizations—included teams as part of their core strategy.

Although many of these fads have faded away, the trend toward both more teams and the use of teams to address more organizational issues has increased dramatically. It seems clear now, in the first decade of the twenty-first century, that teams are not fading away like so many other management fads. Teams and teamwork are here to stay. Equally important, the central unit of the team—the team player—is now widely recognized. The challenge now is how to make teams and team players effective—and that's what this book is all about.

Teams are everywhere. For example, teams are at the core of successful organizational efforts of

- Pharmaceutical companies to develop important new drugs and make them available quickly to patients who need them
- Consumer products companies to improve customer service and speed up the turnaround time on customer requests
- Computer companies to create new systems and software
- Global organizations to collaborate with business partners around the world
- Many old-line companies to redesign and modernize work processes
- Telecommunications companies to improve the quality of products and services
- Manufacturing organizations to reduce costs and eliminate waste
- Schools to coordinate curricula across disciplines
- Sales and marketing organizations to enhance the positioning of brands and coordinate product sales
- Human resources departments who provide consulting support on projects tasked with the design of organizational change efforts
- Some government agencies to reduce cross-functional competition and "turf" conflicts
- Health care systems to coordinate the delivery of quality patient care

Despite all the success, teams and teamwork have been the subject of some serious critical analysis (Robbins and Finley, 1995). Some cynics also joined the chorus of fault-finders, as in the following from an English trade publication:

> Businesses are the grip of a team tyranny. Not simply because work is organized around teams, but because the ethos of *teamworking*—in itself one of those words you feel the English language is not necessarily enriched by—is pervasive. Guff such as 'there is no "I" in team!' surrounds us [Reeves, 2004, p. 29].

However, there is no need now to justify the value of teamwork. In addition, the notion of a team player and the importance of being a team player are accepted ideas in the organizational world. In the earlier edition of this book I described in detail what it means to be a team player. In the past, there had been a rather one-dimensional view of a team player as someone who went along and supported the company program without question—someone who was often described as a "good soldier." A team player, it was said, lived by the credo that "to get along, you go along."

I rejected that view and replaced it with a more complex concept of a team player. It is now clear that a team player cannot be described with a catch phrase, a simple profile, or even a job description. My view, supported by research we conducted at that time, was that there are four types of team players—Contributor, Collaborator, Communicator, and Challenger—each with its own strengths and potential weaknesses. Understanding the four team player styles helps team leaders and members better understand themselves and how they contribute to team success. At the same time I created a survey to help people identify their own styles and thereby gain insight into their individual strengths as well as a means to develop a plan to increase their effectiveness as team players.

The initial version of the instrument, called the *Team Player Survey*, was reprinted in the Resources section of the book. A revised edition was subsequently published in booklet form as the *Parker Team Player Survey* by Xicom in 1991.[1] At the time *Team Players and Teamwork* was first published, I did not anticipate how popular this view of team players would become. In the intervening years, it has been translated into a number of languages and used by organizations around the world, and it has sold more than one million copies. In addition, CRM Learning produced a best-selling video based on the four styles, called *Team Building II: What Makes a Good Team Player?*[2]

As seems clear now, successful organizations place great value on team players. With change the only constant, the successful employees will be the ones who can quickly adjust and work effectively with new and different people. One organizational model that provides some insight into this new world is the movie production crew—a group of people who come together for a brief period of time, work in an intensely collaborative environment, and then deliver a product that is the result of their combined efforts. The successful crew members are able to quickly and easily focus on the goal, share their unique expertise, build relationships with diverse team members, deliver the product on schedule, and then move on. I describe such a person as an *effective team player*. I was witness to this type of teamwork when I was the on-screen narrator of the CRM Learning video that highlighted the four team player styles. The crew, including the various functions—director, cameraperson, sound engineer, teleprompter, make-up, wardrobe, and me—all showed up at 8 A.M. ready to work. Some knew each other from previous projects, but others were meeting their teammates for the first time. They were expected to and did begin work together after little more than a quick cup of coffee.

A key contribution of the first edition was a detailed description of the effective team. Building on the early work of McGregor, Likert, and others, I set forth a list of the twelve characteristics of an effective team. I also created an instrument that gave a team the opportunity to assess their effectiveness against the benchmark of the twelve factors and then the data to begin a team building effort. The initial version of the instrument was printed in the Resources section as the *Team Development Survey*. A revised version was published by Xicom in 1992.[3]

The basic elements of the effective team and team player that I described in 1990 remain the same. The four team player styles and twelve team characteristics still provide effective tools for the team or organization that wants to understand and increase the effectiveness of teamwork and team players. However, the environment in which teams now function has changed in some very important and often dramatic ways.

A team is no longer simply a group of people working in the same area, on the same equipment, with the same customers, and with everyone eating in the same cafeteria. Now our teammates may include people outside of the organization, many of whom we see infrequently, such as customers and suppliers, people in other countries, people in other time zones, and people from other cultures. More specifically, the contextual factors that impact the ability of a team to be successful are numerous.

The changes having the most impact are as follows:

- Teams are cross-functional.
- Teams are cross-cultural.
- Teams are virtual.
- Teams are more dependent on communications technology.
- Team trust is now both more difficult to achieve and more critical to team success.
- Team meetings are more important.
- Teams require a support system.
- Team players serve on multiple teams.
- The level of expectations for teams is much higher.
- Team leadership is both more difficult and more important.

No matter the industry, effective teamwork is critical for success. And teamwork starts with team players—individuals working together to accomplish agreed-upon goals and objectives. Learn what it takes to become an effective team player in a successful team, and the rewards of better products, quality service, reasonable costs, and higher profits will follow.

Background and Purpose of the Book

Team Players and Teamwork provides specific and practical help for people who want to know how to get more team play into their organizations. It provides a clear answer to the question "What is a team player?" In fact, that very question was the genesis of the first edition of the book. It was asked by a manager of a client company in which I was working on ways to improve the performance appraisal system. I pointed out that, although management talked about teamwork throughout the year, it was rarely mentioned during the annual performance appraisal discussions. Somewhat frustrated, one manager asked, "What do we look for? What does a team player really do?" With that question began the journey that culminated in the writing of this book.

The data that form the basis of this book come from a survey of fifty-one companies. Managers and human resource professionals in a variety of industries completed a preliminary open-ended questionnaire. The result of this effort was a structured survey instrument that was mailed to the chief executive officers and vice presidents of human resources of fifty-one companies.

The data indicate that there are many ways a person can be a team player, and positive team process is just one of them. I conceptualized these skills and behaviors into four team player styles that form the heart of *Team Players and Teamwork*. I have expanded the earlier work on teams done by others to create my own model of the effective team and show the many ways in which team players contribute to effective teamwork. And I have enlarged our understanding of leadership by outlining the specific approaches team players use to carry out key leadership functions. A team player can be both a leader and a member. In fact, during the course of a day, a person may occupy both roles as he or she moves from one team to another. But a person's team player style will remain relatively constant even though the expectations placed on him or her will change as the role (leader or member) changes.

In the final analysis, this book is both inspirational and prescriptive. Above all, it should convince the reader of the value of team players and the many ways in which team players can benefit an organization. In addition, the book includes a guide for organizations that want to move toward a team player culture.

Audiences

I wrote *Team Players and Teamwork* with practitioners in mind—leaders in the private, public, and nonprofit sectors who are looking for answers. I see the book as a resource guide on teamwork for people who are ready for something more than exhortation or a compilation of group exercises. *Team Players and Teamwork* is for people who see teamwork as a practical business strategy and want to know how to make it come alive in their organizations. I hope the book will convince readers that team players are critical to the success of the team.

This book is designed for a number of different audiences:

- It will be valuable to business and government leaders who want specific advice on how to change their organizations to increase the quality of teamwork and develop a culture that places a high value on team players. The book includes suggestions drawn from the experience of managers of successful corporations.

- Managers and supervisors who want more team players in their organizations and who want to know what to look for in recruiting, evaluating, and promoting employees will find this book valuable. *Team Players and Teamwork* describes the specific behaviors that characterize team players.

- Human resource and organizational development professionals who want to change their performance management process, reward systems, and organizational culture to emphasize teamwork and team players will find much useful advice here. My detailed descriptions of effective and ineffective team players and the *Parker Team Development Survey* provide the basis for designing successful team assessment and team development interventions.

- Leaders of business unit teams, project teams, task forces, committees, new product teams, sales teams, customer service teams, and other similar teams will find *Team Players and Teamwork* a practical handbook. Leaders will find especially helpful the discussion of the role of the team player as team leader and the methodology for analyzing the strengths and weaknesses of a specific team.

- Team members who want to become more effective team players and increase the effectiveness of their teams will find this book extremely useful. The many checklists, guidelines, and the

Parker Team Player Survey provide the basis for a personal development effort. In addition, the book offers clear advice on increasing team effectiveness at each stage of team development.

- Developers of training programs will find the book a valuable resource for designing workshops in team effectiveness. The book includes an in-depth analysis of the dimensions of an effective team and the role of the team player.

- Students of organizational behavior and human resource development will find *Team Players and Teamwork* a valuable reference. The book acknowledges past contributions to our understanding of teams and adds an important new dimension: the concept of team players. As the business world adopts a teamwork strategy, students and those who plan careers in management will find useful insights here. The first edition of the book was used by a number of team management courses as a textbook.

Overview of the Contents

Team Players and Teamwork begins with a description of the many ways in which team players and teamwork contribute to the success of organizations. Chapter One presents the practical, bottom-line results of teamwork across a variety of industries and occupations. I show how effective teamwork leads to increased productivity, more effective use of resources, cost reduction, improved quality, innovation, better customer service, and more rapid commercialization of products.

Chapter Two provides an in-depth description of the twelve characteristics of an effective team and the role of a team player in bringing each characteristic to life. I discuss the ineffective team and describe the signs of trouble that team leaders can use to detect problems within their teams. I have updated each characteristic to incorporate some of the new realities that have an impact on successful teamwork.

In Chapter Three I depict the four team player styles that form the heart of the book. Using examples from my consulting practice, the survey of fifty-one companies, and the literature, I explain how positive teamwork results from effective team players. Each style description is buttressed by checklists of behaviors and adjectives that will help both leaders and members quickly identify their team player styles. The description of each style is updated to reflect the new challenges faced by team players in the organizational world of the twenty-first century.

Chapter Four begins with an assessment of the organizational costs of ineffective team players. I describe and offer examples of the negative features of each of the four team player styles. The chapter concludes with guidelines for dealing with ineffective team players. Here too I have updated the story to reflect the significant changes in the environment in which teams and team players find themselves today.

Because team leadership is critical to team success, I devote Chapter Five to team players as team leaders. I detail how each of the four team player styles carries out five key leadership functions: planning, communicating, risk taking, problem solving, and decision making. In each case I describe the consequences of ineffective leadership. I also provide team leaders with guidelines for personal development and ten successful team-building strategies. Finally, I address the new issues that confront today's team leader, such as culture, technology, and team composition.

Chapter Six focuses on the four stages of team development—forming, storming, norming, and performing—and how team players successfully adapt to each stage. I describe each stage and pinpoint the key concerns of each team player style. For each stage and style I recommend actions that will help the team grow and develop into a mature, adaptable organization.

Chapter Seven provides team leaders with a methodology for analyzing the strengths and weaknesses of their teams. I discuss the consequences of having too many people with the same team player style. I also describe the dangers inherent in a team that is missing one of the four styles. Several sample team profiles are presented as a self-study exercise in team assessment.

In Chapter Eight I offer a prescription to organizational leaders who want to create an environment that encourages teamwork and values team players. Drawing on examples provided by our survey respondents, I describe a variety of methods used by successful organizations. Job assignments, promotional policies, performance management, team awards, and team player recognition are among the many techniques outlined in this chapter.

The final chapter presents a series of challenges to leaders, managers, human resource professionals, and training specialists who see team players and teamwork as the centerpiece of their competitive business strategy.

A Resources section includes the *Parker Team-Development Survey* and the *Parker Team Player Survey*. The *Parker Team-Development Survey* helps a team assess its strengths and weaknesses in terms of the twelve characteristics of an effective team. The *Parker Team Player Survey* is an instrument that helps an individual identify his or her primary team player style. The section also includes a report that presents frequency data on the extent to which each team player style occurs in the business world.

Glenn M. Parker
Skillman, New Jersey
October 2007

Notes

1. Xicom is now a subsidiary of CPP, Inc. The survey is now available from www.cpp.com.

2. For more information, see www.crmlearning.com.

3. Now distributed by CPP, Inc. (www.cpp.com).

The Author

Author and consultant Glenn M. Parker works with organizations to create and sustain high performing teams, effective team players, and team-based systems. His first book, *Team Players and Teamwork* (Jossey-Bass, 1990), became a best-seller and was selected as one of the ten best business books of 1990. Key concepts from the book were brought to the screen in the best-selling video *Team Building II: What Makes a Good Team Player?* (CRM Films, 1995). His training and team building instrument, the *Parker Team Player Survey* (Xicom/CPP, 1991, 2003), has sold more than one million copies. Glenn is one of only seventy-five management experts recognized in *The Guru Guide* (Wiley, 1998).

A revised and updated edition of Glenn's major best-seller *Cross-Functional Teams: Working with Allies, Enemies, and Other Strangers* was published by Jossey-Bass/Wiley in 2003. He is coauthor of *50 Activities for Team Building*, Vol. 1 (HRD Press, 1991), which was selected by *Human Resource Executive* as one of 1992's Top Ten Training Tools. Glenn is also coauthor of *50 Activities for Self-Directed Teams* (HRD Press, 1994) and editor of the HRD Press *Best Practices for Teams*, Vol. 1 (1996) and Vol. 2 (1998). Other publications include *25 Instruments for Team Building* (HRD Press, 1998), *Teamwork: 20 Steps for Building Powerful Teams* (Successories, 1998), *Teamwork and Teamplay: Games and Activities for Training and Building Teams* (Pfeiffer, 1999), *Rewarding Teams: Lessons from the Trenches* (Jossey-Bass, 2000), *Team Depot: A Warehouse of 585 Tools to Rejuvenate Your Team* (Pfeiffer, 2002), and *Meeting Excellence: 33 Tools to Lead Meetings That Get Results* (Jossey-Bass, 2006).

Glenn does not just talk or write about teamwork. He is a hands-on consultant and trainer who works with startup and ongoing teams of all types in a variety of industries. He facilitates team building, conducts training workshops, consults with management, and gives presentations for organizations across a wide variety of industries. His clients have included pharmaceutical companies such as Novartis, Merck and Company, Johnson & Johnson, Bristol-Myers Squibb, Hoffmann-La Roche, Aventis, Novo Nordisk, and contract research organizations; a variety of industrial organizations such as 3M, Kimberly-Clark, The Budd Company, Penntech Papers, Allied Signal, Pratt & Whitney, LEGO, BOC Gases, and Sun Microsystems; companies in telecommunications including AT&T, Pacific Bell, NYNEX, Lucent/Bell Labs, Telcordia Technologies (formerly Bellcore), and Siemens/ROLM Communications; service businesses such as Commerce Clearing House's Legal Information Service, Asea Brown Boveri (ABB) Environmental Services, American Express, Promus Hotel Corporation (Embassy Suites, Hampton Inns), CDI Corp., and the *New England Journal of Medicine;* the sales and marketing organizations of Roche Laboratories and the Pontiac Division of General Motors; health care providers such as Palomar-Pomerado Health System, Pocono Medical Center, St. Rita's Medical Center, Monmouth Medical Center, and Riverside Health Care Center; retailers such as Ann Taylor and Phillips-Van Heusen; as well as teams from government agencies at the Environmental Protection Agency, National Institutes of Health, Department of the Navy, and the U.S. Coast Guard.

Glenn holds a bachelor of arts degree from City College of New York and a master of arts degree from the University of Illinois and has studied for the doctorate at Cornell University. He is much in demand as a speaker at corporate meetings and at international professional conferences in human resources, team development, and project management.

Glenn is the father of three grown children and lives with his wife, Judy, in central New Jersey. In his spare time, he roots for the Philadelphia 76ers, rides his bike, and plans his next vacation. As an active volunteer with the American Cancer Society, he helped create Run for Dad, an event to raise awareness about prostate cancer, which annually raises thousands of dollars and draws some 1,500 runners, walkers, and children on Father's Day.

1

TEAM PLAYERS AND TEAMWORK: THE NEW REALITY

In the 1980s many highly regarded books on business leadership highlighted the value of teamwork and team players (Kanter, 1983; Peters, 1987; Bradford and Cohen, 1984; Lawler, 1986). In the real world, however, team building was more promoted by behavioral scientists than it was accepted and practiced in American business. Teamwork was considered "nice" but not critical for the success of the corporation. Teamwork as a goal was linked with other corporate goals that were given more lip service than real backing—goals such as community responsibility, affirmative action, a clean environment, and employee development.

Then, at the end of that decade, teamwork gained in importance as public and private sector leaders saw the tangible benefits of effective programs. Global competition, workforce changes, the impact of technology, and other factors pushed organizations in the United States to experiment with team approaches to achieving cost-effective, quality products and services.

A few solid examples from that era are instructive:

> Honeywell's commercial flight division in Minneapolis, devoted largely to manufacturing our navigational systems, switched to team organization about six years ago. Virtually all plant functions, including production, conflict resolution, even allocation of funds, is done by teams . . . [As a result] Honeywell's Minneapolis plant has 80 percent of the flight-navigational systems market, and 1988 profits were 200 percent above projections [Chance, 1989, p. 18].

GEMICO's [General Electric Mortgage Insurance Company] experience in its Seattle office dramatically illustrates the benefits realized by creating a teamwork mentality. During 1985, GEMICO's market share in Washington hit an all-time low and delinquencies and loan declinations skyrocketed due to deteriorating business quality. At the beginning of 1986, faced with the prospect of withdrawing from the state, GEMICO's branch manager and newly-hired experienced sales representatives began to work together to turn the situation around. First, everyone agreed that their goal would be to increase the volume of quality business received from Washington lenders. Second, everyone on the team demonstrated a willingness to "wear different hats" to see this task accomplished. Sales reps met with lenders to discuss underwriting problems, and supported (rather than second-guessed) underwriters when loans were declined. At the same time, branch office underwriters accompanied sales reps on customer calls, and loan processors served as unofficial customer service reps. The result: GEMICO market share in Washington has more than doubled, while loan declinations have been cut in half and delinquency rates have dropped from 3.05 percent to 2.52 percent, lower than the average for all mortgage insurers [Barmore, 1987, p. 94].

At Xerox headquarters in Rochester, New York, on a typical work day they [encoders] process about 6,000 customer payment checks worth about $6 million. With that level of volume, operators were frequently so overwhelmed that checks were left undeposited until the next time, watering down the company's return on assets.

Xerox encourages team problem solving—even awarding those groups that find new ways to cut costs or improve quality—so that's what the encoders did. They formed a team and set to work analyzing the problem.

The encoders found that productivity, morale, and communication were better on Saturdays than any other of the six work days. The reason: work flow was managed through a coordinator Monday through Friday, leaving the encoders little control over what got processed, by whom, or when. On Saturdays, when the encoders had to distribute their work, assign machines, and juggle their lunch breaks themselves, workflow was far better. The end result: The coordinator position was eliminated. Now the encoders form a "huddle" twice daily at mail delivery time to divide the work. In one month, they found a 21 percent reduction in the number of checks carried over to the next business day, a 70 percent decrease in overtime, $7000 in ROA improvements, and immeasurable improvement in employee morale, communication, and employee involvement ["Copy Cats Worth Copying," 1988, p. 28].

Cheesebrough-Ponds used a high-intensity task force to reformulate and reposition its Rave Home Permanent product as Rave Moisturelock Perm. Management organized a team which included the brand group, research and development, packaging and the agency account group [Feder and Mitchell, 1988, p. 21].

Pratt and Whitney used special teams to reinvigorate its production capability by reconfiguring its engine manufacturing operations into numerous small units [Herman and Herman, 1989, p. 90].

Keithley Instruments' plant in Salem, Ohio, saw output increase by 90 percent and absenteeism fall by 75 percent when its production teams went to work [Chance, 1989, p. 18].

A five-part management plan provided the framework for management improvement in the Department of Agriculture. Much of the credit goes to an emphasis on innovation and the cooperative effort of many employees [Franke, 1988–89, p. 11].

A recent study reported schools that have team management outperform schools that have hierarchical management (Chubb, 1988). For example, many school districts in Marin County, California, are encouraging a team-based effort which, among other things, schedules time for teachers and staff to work together and share decision making at all levels (Lambert, 1989).

In other areas, management, workers, and, often, unions teamed up to regain and maintain the competitive edge. Quality circles passed through the fad stage and were used as a strategy for changing the cultures at many companies and government agencies. Fundamentally, the quality-circle approach is a team-based strategy for improving quality and reducing costs. On the heels of quality circles came the total-quality approach ("do it right the first time") advocated by Philip Crosby (1979) and implemented at scores of companies across the country. One of the most dramatic efforts to meet the global challenge was the cooperation of Japanese and American auto manufacturers and U.S. trade unionists. During this era the New United Motor Manufacturing Inc. (NUMMI) joint venture of Toyota and General Motors, with the United Automobile Workers as the bargaining agent, was the most famous example. "In just four years, it has achieved productivity and quality levels that exceed anything in the American auto industry, and which rival Japan's best" (Lee, 1988).

Many other automobile companies followed the Japanese lead and implemented team production. For example, at the Mazda Motor Manufacturing (USA) plant in Flat Rock, Michigan, the team method meant "Workers learn several jobs and are expected to participate in problem-solving" (Kertesz, 1988, p. 36). Another 1980s team experiment that was closely watched by American automakers was the Volvo plant that opened in Uddevalla, Sweden, in which Volvo traded the traditional assembly line for self-managed work teams of seven to ten employees. "Each team works in one area and assembles four cars per shift. Since members are trained to handle all assembly jobs, they work an average of three hours before repeating the same task" (Kapstein and Hoerr, 1989, p. 92).

It's the Twenty-First Century: Team Players and Teamwork Are Here to Stay

Toward the end of the twentieth century the agenda changed. We were no longer justifying the value of teamwork or presenting case examples of successful teams. So the battle was over, and we had won. Teamwork was established as a critical aspect of business strategy. Team players were considered valued partners in the process. It was clear that effective teamwork can produce tangible benefits for people and organizations:

- New products get to the market faster.
- Customers get better service.
- Employees are more satisfied.
- The quality of products and services increases.
- The cost of production decreases.
- There are fewer lost-time accidents.
- Students learn better.
- Creativity and innovation are enhanced.

The discussion has now shifted to tools for sustainability of high performing teams—how to do it right every time. The case examples from Xerox, GE, Honeywell, and others cited earlier in this chapter proved that teams could produce clear, measurable results. Now the challenge became how to create a model and tools to develop teams in the trenches. Then, in the 1990s, came the work of several researchers and thought leaders who provided various perspectives on how to develop and sustain an effective team.

Following my work on team players and teamwork came a breakthrough book by Katzenbach and Smith (1993), providing data from fifty teams in thirty companies and demonstrating the critical difference between high performing teams and other teams: the successful teams had "clear performance objectives." Although I had previously identified a "clear purpose" as one of the twelve characteristics of an effective team (see Chapter Two), Katzenbach and Smith proved that it was *the most important characteristic*. In the same era, Larson and LaFasto (1989) analyzed a wide variety of successful teams and emerged with a list of eight characteristics of effectively functioning teams.

My colleague, Jack Zigon, did some great work on tools for measuring team effectiveness (1999). Another colleague and friend, Jerry McAdams, wrote the best book on recognition and rewards (1996), and Dave Jamieson did a masterful job of describing the elements of a team-based strategy (1996). The first edition of my book on cross-functional teams presented the first comprehensive examination of this growing teamwork trend. The book has since been revised and updated to include many of the emerging elements of the new team landscape (Parker, 2003).

While all this research and writing was taking place, the world of team players and teamwork was changing right under our noses. The environmental conditions in which teams were asked to perform were changing in a rather dramatic fashion. And these changes were not making life any easier for teams; rather, it was becoming significantly more difficult to develop and sustain an effective team over time. It is important to understand these changes in order to update and adapt the characteristics of an effective team and the team player styles.

Team Members Are Located in Multiple Locations. In the era of global organizations it is not unusual for a team to be composed of people from company sites in Asia, Europe, and the Americas. For example, I recently facilitated a team building meeting for a team that included members from Brazil, Italy, France, Switzerland, England, Germany, Japan, and the United States. There are a number of consequences of this factor:

- Communication is more difficult because of language differences.
- Communication is more difficult because of cultural differences.
- Communication is more difficult because of the inherent limitations of electronic communications technology.

- Informal interactions among teammates that quite naturally occur in the hallway, cafeteria, and offices on a colocated team do not take place.
- Team players have to be more assertive in developing effective relationships with their teammates who are located in other sites.

Many Meetings Use Teleconferencing, Videoconferencing, or Web Conferencing Technology. Because most teams require weekly or monthly meetings and members are not colocated, meetings must, of necessity, use teleconferencing technology, videoconferencing if it is available, or a web-based tool, if one can be found that meets the needs of the team. This factor creates the following consequences:

- There is limited or no visual or nonverbal communication.
- There are often breakdowns in the operation of the technology.
- Being an effective team player now requires an ability to communicate with people who are not in the same room.
- Being an effective team leader now requires a capability to make effective use of the new technology.

There Are Cultural Differences Among Team Members. With teams composed of members from different countries, members bring to the experience a wide variety of communication styles, approaches to decision making, and attitudes toward leadership. This factor creates the following consequences:

- There are misunderstandings that sometimes lead to conflict and negative feelings.
- Being a team player now includes understanding and working with people who are culturally different.

- It is more likely that deadlines are missed and progress toward team goals does not meet expectations.
- It is now incumbent upon the team leader to ensure that the channels of communication are appropriate for people with different communication styles.

The Bar Has Been Raised for Team Success. As teams have become an established part of organization strategy, it is expected that all teams will function at a high level. This is especially true in organizations where there has been a heavy investment in team development services such as training and consulting. These are the consequences:

- There is a greater impatience among senior management when they see lack of team progress.
- There is added pressure on team leaders to demonstrate progress, which can result in lowering the bar on quality, forgoing good team practices, and increasing the stress on team members.
- Being a successful team leader now requires regular and effective communication with senior management to manage the expectations of the team.
- Being an effective team player increases the importance of challenging conventional thinking to ensure the best possible team outcome.

There Is Recognition That Team Success Requires a Support System. Progressive organizations have come to realize that simply creating teams is not enough to ensure success. It is now clear that there is a need for a total system that includes a supportive management style, performance management process, reward systems, and a team-based culture. These are the consequences:

- There is a search for new and creative ways of looking at how leaders are selected, members are appraised, and teams are rewarded.

- The organization must shift to a more fluid structure that facilitates cross-functional collaboration.

- Senior management must adopt a style that is supportive of team players.

- There must be a conscious effort to alter the culture to one that values team players, encourages collaboration across functions, and rewards teamwork.

- The organization must adopt new methods for rewarding successful teams, recognizing outstanding team players, and incorporating performance on a team into the overall employee appraisal process.

There Is More Cross-Functional Teaming. As my earlier work (Parker, 2003) shows, the new world of business demands that an increasing number of teams be composed of people from many different functional organizations. It is no longer possible, for example, to develop complex new products, provide quality customer service, and close major sales with large clients without a coordinated approach among people from a variety of disciplines. This factor has the following implications:

- The job of team leader becomes more difficult because of the need to coordinate the work of people who may have different goals, work styles, and commitment to the team, with little or no authority to influence or control their actions.

- There is a greater need for adaptive team players on the team who are able to quickly develop trust, communicate with people who are different, and subordinate their functional goals to the goals of the team.

- There is an increased need for team training in such areas as meeting facilitation, conflict resolution, and communications skills in order to help teams take advantage of all the resources on the team.

The Team Leader's Role Is Both More Important and More Difficult. With many more teams being cross-functional, cross-cultural, and virtual, the demands on the leader have increased exponentially. It is simply more challenging to provide leadership when the members of the team report to a functional manager, are culturally different, and work in distant company locations. This factor has the following implications:

- It is critical that the leader have the requisite interpersonal skills to work with a diverse team membership.
- It is essential that the leader have high level influence skills to offset the lack of direct management authority over the members of the team.
- It is very important that senior management have a rational process in place for the selection of team leaders.
- The leader must have excellent diplomacy skills in order to develop and maintain effective relationships with a variety of stakeholders, including corporate leadership, department heads, support groups, and external regulatory bodies as well as suppliers and other vendors.

Successful Team Meeting Management Is Now Even More Critical. Meetings are still the most visible team activity. And, given the new reality of teams that are virtual, cross-cultural, and cross-functional, the degree of difficulty in achieving a successful meeting has significantly increased. The challenge for team leaders—and, yes, for team members as well—is to ensure that the increasing amount of time (and the corresponding costs) spent in meetings produces something of value. Implications of this factor include the following:

- Team leaders need high-level meeting facilitation skills or access to training that provides these skills.
- Team members need orientation or training in the skills of being an effective meeting participant. They also need to

feel equally responsible for accomplishing the meeting's objectives.

- Team members and leaders need easy access to a kit of tools, templates, and checklists for planning and managing a successful meeting.
- Senior management needs to set the standard for effective meeting management by using all the right tools and demonstrating high-level meeting facilitation skills.

Building Trust Quickly Is Now Even More Essential to Effective Teamwork. Because diversity—functional, cultural, and geographical—is now the norm on so many teams, the potential for communications breakdowns based on lack of trust is great. With limited opportunity to overcome barriers and build trust through regular face-to-face meetings and informal contacts such as hallway conversations, lunch, and coffee breaks, trust building has become a major challenge. This has the following implications:

- Effective open communication based on a high level of trust may take longer than usual.
- Teams may have to adopt the norm of *swift trust,* whereby members assume their teammates are trustworthy from the outset of their relationship (Myerson, Weick, and Kramer, 1996).
- Trust building exercises will need to be an integral part of a project kickoff meeting.

People Serve on Multiple Teams. In the new world of cross-functional teaming, it is not unusual for subject matter experts to be a member of three or four teams—I have known at least one person who was on six teams! Some of these people can spend a good part of a workday simply going from meeting to meeting, resulting in an oft-heard complaint: "I can't get any work done because I'm in meetings all day." These are the consequences of this factor:

- It is more difficult to develop a positive team spirit because many members have divided loyalties.
- It is more difficult to get team tasks completed because many members have conflicting work priorities.
- It more difficult to schedule team meetings and to get people to attend meetings because meeting times often conflict with each other.
- For obvious multiple reasons, it is stressful for team members.

In this chapter we have described a number of important changes in the landscape in which many teams find themselves in the twenty-first century. We have also addressed the implications of these changes for the ability of organizations, teams, team leaders, and team players to be successful in this new world. In the chapters that follow we will build on our basic concepts of the effective team and team players by incorporating tools to address these new realities of teamwork in the twenty-first century.

2

WHAT MAKES A TEAM EFFECTIVE OR INEFFECTIVE

Teams are everywhere. In business we have new product teams, quality teams, and project teams. In sports we have offensive teams, defensive teams, first teams, second teams, special teams, and all-star teams. In the arts a team is referred to in a variety of ways, including cast, crew, ensemble, company, and troupe. In politics we have party, caucus, coalition, committee, and council.

Teams have an important place in our professional and personal lives. But not every group is a team and not every team is effective. In fact, one of our great frustrations is the failure of teams to function smoothly. This can be seen in comments such as "We need to act more like a team," "The only way we can succeed is to work more like a team," and "We need more team players."

A group of people is not a team. A team is a group of people with a high degree of interdependence geared toward the achievement of a goal or completion of a task. In other words, they agree on a goal and agree that the only way to achieve the goal is to work together.

My colleague and friend Bill Fox, formerly an executive with Telcordia Technologies, Inc., and now managing partner of Vanguard Communications, amplifies this definition with a good sports analogy: "The ten thousand runners in the New York City marathon race have a common goal or purpose. However, they are not a team. They are, in fact, in competition with each other. Teamwork requires interdependence—the working together of a group of people with a shared objective. More specifically, the only way the runners can reach their goal is by competitive efforts."

Using another track example, Fox argues that a relay team is a good example of a real team. All members of the team share a common goal, and they must work together to achieve it. All members of an 800-meter relay team must do their part by running fast, passing the baton skillfully, and encouraging each other. Although one person could win the 800-meter distance, a team of four people each responsible for 200 meters will win most of the time. The potential for teamwork exists in the relay team. However, success will be dependent on the degree to which they behave like an effective team.

Teamwork: Lessons from the Past

Our approach to the dimensions of an effective team grows out of and builds on a base of theory and research in behavioral science. Although we owe a debt to a few seminal thinkers in group dynamics, our approach is more comprehensive and appropriate for the new look of teamwork and team players in today's world of global organizations.

In the 1920s Elton Mayo uncovered the importance of teams and the power of the informal system in the workplace during his most famous research project, conducted at the Hawthorne works of Western Electric Company in Chicago (Pugh and Hickson, 1989). The informal system that Mayo identified persists today as an organizational issue under the rubric of *culture*. However, the issues and the teams today are broader and more complex than those studied by Mayo and his colleagues.

During the 1930s Kurt Lewin focused attention on the behavior of groups and on the forces that help to explain the actions of groups. Lewin's work led to the development of a field of study known as *group dynamics*. His unique contribution was called *force field analysis*, and it helped us understand what people can do to increase the effectiveness of teams (Lewin, 1951).

In Lewin's view, a team is an open social system with a series of forces or vectors applied to it from two sides. If the forces are equal, the team will remain in a state of equilibrium—it will not change. However, if the forces on one side increase or decrease, the balance point will change. Force field analysis is still used today as a technique for improving the effectiveness of teams.

About twenty years later, Douglas McGregor and his colleagues began studying the development of managers in industry. The study culminated in the publication of *The Human Side of Enterprise* (McGregor, 1960), one of the most important books of our time. Most of the book is devoted to an explanation of a set of assumptions about motivation that McGregor labeled *Theory X* and *Theory Y*. However, in the last chapter, McGregor presented lists of the characteristics of effective and ineffective management teams. These lists have had almost as much influence as Theory X and Theory Y. McGregor's Effective Team can be summarized as follows:

- The atmosphere tends to be informal, comfortable, and relaxed.
- There is a lot of discussion in which virtually everyone participates.
- The task or the objective of the group is well understood and accepted by the members.
- The members listen to each other.
- There is disagreement but the group is comfortable with this.
- Most decisions are reached by consensus.
- Criticism is frequent, frank, and relatively comfortable.
- People are free in expressing their feelings as well as their ideas, both on the problem and on the group's operation.
- When action is taken, clear assignments are made and accepted.
- The leader of the team does not dominate discussions.
- Frequently, [the team] will stop to examine how well it is doing or what may be interfering with its operation.

Another influential person was psychologist Rensis Likert, who established the Institute for Social Research at the University of Michigan. Likert studied managers and supervisors with the best performance records to find out what worked and why (Likert, 1961). He found that the least effective managers were "job centered" whereas the most effective were "employee centered." Likert summarized his findings into four systems of management. System 4, the most effective approach, produced high productivity and greater employee involvement. Today, we would characterize System 4 as participative or team management. Likert's list of the twenty-four characteristics of an effective team is similar to McGregor's formulation in that the focus is on the process or internal dynamics of the team.

The psychologist Chris Argyris focused his attention on the personal development of the individual in the context of the organization. Organizational effectiveness, Argyris believed, was a function of the interpersonal competence of team members and the extent to which the organization supported positive norms (1964, pp. 139–140). He enumerated positive team norms as follows:

1. To be candid about ideas and feelings
2. To be open
3. To experiment
4. To help others to be candid about their ideas and feelings
5. To help others to be open
6. To help others to experiment
7. Individuality
8. Thought
9. Concern
10. Internal commitment

Argyris pointed to the team-member behaviors required for effective teamwork. Although his focus was also on internal process, his emphasis on candor, experimentation, and individuality was helpful in giving emphasis to the need for team players who are willing to challenge the status quo.

The work of Robert Blake and Jane Mouton is extremely important because it links management style and team effectiveness in a concept called the Managerial Grid model (Blake and Mouton, 1964). In the upper right-hand corner of the Grid is the 9.9 manager. This style is characterized by a high concern for both people (process) and production (task). A person with this style emphasizes fact-finding and an open discussion of issues as the keys to effective problem solving and decision making. A team of 9.9 people will work interdependently and will seek full commitment to their decision before proceeding. Today, we would refer to this team as *performing* or *high performing* (see Chapter Six).

The Grid is used to improve overall team effectiveness as well as the individual effectiveness of each team member. Grid team building involves an analysis of the current team criteria in terms of planning, problem solving, communication, and other dimensions of an effective team in the context of the Grid. Team building also includes feedback from team members on their perceptions of each person's Grid style in actual team situations. Structured experiences help team members apply this information, and the net result of this phase of Grid development is a plan for team and individual improvement. Blake and Mouton gave us a model of team excellence and a set of styles useful in understanding team-member contributions.

In the same period Bruce Tuckman (1965) published an article in an obscure journal about a series of predictable stages that a typical team will experience. The impact of Tuckman's four stages—forming, storming, norming, and performing—endures to this day. In Chapter Six you will find a detailed description of each stage along with specific advice for team players on how they can help their team advance to the high performing stage.

Other contributions have been helpful in understanding teamwork and team players. Richard Walton (1969) provided a helpful distinction between types of conflict that may arise among team members. Substantive conflict involves disagreements about roles, procedures, and policies and can be dealt with by discussion and negotiation. Emotional conflict arises from feelings of loss, fear, and mistrust. Although there is often overlap, it is helpful to identify the underlying causes of internal team conflicts. Role analysis and role negotiation are two techniques designed to deal with conflicts of this type (Dayal and Thomas, 1968; Harrison, 1971). William Dyer's (1987) *Team Building: Issues and Alternatives* was one of the most influential books in the field because it included a variety of techniques for managers and consultants who facilitate team-building events. Beginning in the 1970s, William Pfeiffer and John Jones pioneered the publication of reproducible materials for team building facilitators with their various handbooks (see www.pfeiffer.com).

Following closely on the heels of my work on team player styles and the effective team came the research on team effectiveness by two McKinsey consultants, Jon Katzenbach and Douglas Smith (1993). Katzenbach and Smith showed that high performing teams were distinguished by a set of specific performance objectives.

As we acknowledge the more important contributions by behavioral scientists and others, it is necessary to note that the organizational environment has changed rather dramatically. As we described in the previous chapter, new and decidedly more challenging demands are being placed on teams and team players. Therefore, we need to adapt our model of effective teamwork to factors such as these:

- The level of expectations for teams has significantly increased.
- Many more teams are now global in scope.
- Team members are often not colocated.
- More teams are cross-functional.
- Teams are often culturally diverse.
- There are new requirements for a system of supports for teams.
- Building trust and open communication is more challenging.
- Teams make greater use of communications technology.

A New Model of Team Effectiveness

Twelve characteristics or behaviors distinguish effective teams from ineffective teams. You get a certain feeling when you are part of a solid team. You enjoy being around the people, you look forward to all meetings, you learn new things, you laugh more, you find yourself putting the team's assignments ahead of other work, and you feel a real sense of progress and accomplishment. In the final analysis, effective teams are composed of effective team players. The twelve characteristics of an effective team come alive when team members are high performing team players. In this chapter, we outline the characteristics of an effective team and the role of team players. Table 2.1 presents a summary of the characteristics, which are more fully explored in the text that follows. In the next chapter we present four team player styles and discuss how each contributes to effective teamwork.

Table 2.1 Characteristics of an Effective Team

1. Clear Purpose	The vision, mission, goal, or task of the team has been defined and is now accepted by everyone. There is an action plan.
2. Informality	The climate tends to be informal, comfortable, and relaxed. There are no obvious tensions or signs of boredom.
3. Participation	There is much discussion and everyone is encouraged to participate.
4. Listening	The members use effective listening techniques such as questioning, paraphrasing, and summarizing to get out ideas.
5. Civilized Disagreement	There is disagreement, but the team is comfortable with this and shows no signs of avoiding, smoothing over, or suppressing conflict.
6. Consensus Decision	For important decisions, the goal is substantial but not necessarily unanimous agreement through open discussion of everyone's ideas and avoidance of formal voting or easy compromises.

(continued)

Table 2.1 (*continued*)

7. Open Communication and Trust	Team members feel free to express their opinions on the tasks as well as on the group's operation, coupled with a high level of trust. Communication also takes place outside of meetings.
8. Clear Roles and Work Assignments	There are clear expectations about the roles played by each team member. When action is taken, clear assignments are made, accepted, and carried out. Work is fairly distributed among team members.
9. Shared Leadership	Although the team has a formal leader, leadership functions shift from time to time depending on the circumstances, the needs of the group, and the skills of the members. The formal leader models the appropriate behavior and helps establish positive norms.
10. External Relations	The team spends time developing key outside relationships, mobilizing resources, and building credibility with important players in other parts of the organization.
11. Style Diversity	The team has a broad spectrum of team player types, including members who emphasize attention to task, goal setting, focus on process, and questions about how the team is functioning.
12. Self-Assessment	Periodically, the team stops to examine how well it is functioning and what may be interfering with its effectiveness.

Clear Sense of Purpose

Call it a mission, goal, objective, or task, but a team must know why it exists and what it should be doing at the end of a meeting, by the end of the quarter, at year's end, or perhaps five years from now. There are few more frustrating activities than being part of a group (masquerading as a team) that meets with no sense of why they have come together. In some organizations, employees are part of a unit because of what I call *administrative convenience*.

Everyone has to be somewhere in the company's hierarchy, but sometimes the rationale for the placement is not clear.

In a team-building session, a division management team spent three days building and formulating their mission—a statement outlining their basic products and services and their principal customers. Although the meetings that led to the mission statement were difficult and tiring, operating without a shared understanding of the team's purpose would have been significantly more frustrating. No one likes to be part of something that is not going anywhere. Subsequently, the team went on to develop goals, objectives, and tasks.

In today's fast-paced world, most teams do not have three days to devote to the creation of a mission statement. In the case of project teams, the kickoff meeting will involve the development of a charter, including roles and responsibilities. This chartering process is followed closely by the formation of a project plan. IBM, for example, calls it a *statement of work* (see "Case Study 2: A Virtual Cross-Functional Team Story" in Parker, 2003, pp. 247–261). The statement of work or project plan may include some or all of the following sections:

- Overarching goal or purpose
- Statement of need or problem that needs to be addressed
- Specific objectives or outcomes
- Timetable of key events or milestones
- Deliverables
- Resource needs
- Budget or cost estimate

Katzenbach and Smith (1993), in their seminal study of some fifty teams in thirty companies, concluded that "the best teams invest a tremendous amount of time and effort exploring, shaping, and agreeing on a purpose that belongs to them both collectively and individually" (p. 50).

Similarly, Larson and LaFasto (1989), in their examination of a very diverse sample of some 75 teams, found that ". . . in *every case*, without exception, when an effectively functioning team was identified, it was described by the respondent as having a clear understanding of the objective" (emphasis added, p. 27).

Today's global organizations are insisting on very specific team outcomes or performance objectives tied to specific target dates. As a result, some companies and government agencies are going back to an old classic, the SMART objectives model, shown in Figure 2.1.

Effective teams are also clear about their short-term tasks. Although it is important to create a shared mission and project plan, the success of most teams is dependent on their ability to focus on the task at hand. Therefore, successful teams keep that next deadline or deliverable at the top of their agenda. In fact, one project team leader whose work I respect always begins each meeting with a snapshot of the project plan that highlights the current timeline on the screen. In this way, team members are reminded of what they need to do and when they need to do it.

Figure 2.1 Smart Objectives Model

S . . . . Specific

M . . . . Measurable*

A . . . . Attainable

R . . . . Relevant

T . . . . Time-bound

*or Observable

With this exercise she also lets members know the consequences of failure to produce action items on time or get needed commitments and significant changes, particularly additions to the project plan.

Goals are powerful psychological motivators of action by team members. "If we have a goal before us and think that with a little more effort we could achieve it, we're excited by the challenge. When we've made some progress, we realize that the effort has paid off, and we experience a small sense of triumph. And then we're confronted by the next step—a new challenge—and the desire kicks in again" (Klein, 2002, p. 224). The message here is that it is important to divide a large, long-term goal into a series of short-term objectives, tasks, or deliverables. With this strategy, team members can experience the satisfaction of success at various milestones along the way, and the team can keep members motivated to keep going. We also suggest team rewards—even informal rewards such as pizza or a cake at a meeting when a milestone is reached. This may also be a good time to recognize individual team members who made a special contribution to the accomplishment of the objective.

The concept of a clear purpose also extends to the team meeting (Parker and Hoffman, 2006). In our workshop, *Building a Meeting Facilitator's Tool Kit*, team leaders learn to open every meeting with a clear statement of the "key meeting outcome." The general guideline is NO PURPOSE = NO MEETING!! Therefore, meeting facilitators are encouraged to begin the meeting with something like these examples:

- "Good morning and welcome to today's meeting of the ABXY Project Team. The key meeting outcome of today's meeting is to develop a plan to address the . . . Now let's review the agenda."
- "Welcome to the monthly meeting of the OnCon 320 Team. By the end of this meeting we need to complete the final section of the marketing plan."

The importance of a clear purpose cannot be overemphasized. In today's world, with people on multiple teams and stretched to the limit, organizations cannot afford to waste their time. More important, team members resent being part of a team that lacks a clear direction or attending meetings that have no focus. Recent survey results at a major pharmaceutical company revealed that one of the biggest complaints was that so many meetings were a waste of time.

Team players play an important role in creating a clear sense of purpose by

- Insisting that the team have clear goals and objectives and periodically revisit them
- Creating milestone charts with specific deliverables
- Ensuring the involvement of all members in development of the team's purpose
- Pushing the team to reach for "stretch" goals and objectives
- Asking that every team meeting have a key meeting outcome and an agenda

Informal Climate

The atmosphere in an effective team tends to be informal, comfortable, and relaxed. There are no obvious signs of boredom or tension. One signal that your team is effective is that you enjoy being around the people. You want to come to the team meetings. You look forward to all associations and contacts with other team members. You know the feeling because you have had the opposite feeling so many times. When you are part of a poorly functioning team, your reaction to receiving the meeting notice is usually something like "Ugh." You dread the team get-togethers and find yourself looking for excuses to avoid the meetings and other contacts with team members.

A team with a positive climate bypasses the formal trappings such as rigid voting rules and raising hands before speaking.

Rather, an obvious ease of interaction and communication relaxes team members and enhances their contributions. Members feel comfortable speaking with each other regardless of position, age, sex, or race.

On new global teams with culturally diverse memberships, it may take more work to develop an informal climate. If team meetings are held via teleconference or video conference, creating a more relaxed environment may take a focused effort by the team leader. For example, we suggest that these meetings begin with some informal conversation about such topics as the weather, current news, or member's vacation plans.[1] For global teams we strongly recommend at least one face-to-face meeting a year in which members can "put a name with a face" and get to know each other better as they conduct team business, participate in team building exercises, and hold informal evening events.

Humor seems to be an integral part of successful teams. Members talk about team meetings as "enjoyable" and "fun" and even "a lot of laughs." When the environment is relaxed and informal, people feel free to engage in good-natured kidding, social banter about events unrelated to work, and anecdotes regarding recent company business. Some psychological studies indicate that friendly gestures such as verbal compliments or small fun gifts like candy can increase creativity and effective problem solving (Isen and others, 1987). In our facilitation skills workshops for team leaders we suggest the periodic use of small items such as candy, funny playthings, and stress toys.[2] However, keep in mind that it is the surprise that makes it effective. If you use these items at every meeting, the effect will soon be lost.

Look around at some of your best teams and assess the degree of formality. You will notice that team members often come early to the meetings because they enjoy the informal chatting over coffee prior to the meeting. And the pleasant looks on members' faces are indicators that they enjoy being there. After the meeting, they will usually stay for a while to continue the discussion or just to trade stories. I have noticed that effective teams schedule meetings at times that facilitate the informal aspects. For example:

- First thing in the morning, beginning with time for coffee and socializing
- Just prior to noon, followed by a lunch together
- At the end of the day, followed by an informal get-together at a nearby restaurant

We cannot end this discussion without a note of caution. Jokes are usually culture-specific and therefore do not translate well into another language. So although it is desirable to inject humor (as opposed to a joke) into a team meeting, it needs to be done carefully and with sensitivity to both cultural and language differences among members. In addition, some team members representing certain areas of the world (Asia-Pacific, for example) are used to and expect a formal meeting in which hierarchical relationships are the norm. Therefore, it may take some time, some careful planning, and even some team building activities to develop an informal climate on your team.

Team players help create an informal climate by

- Offering to provide the team with the necessary resources without waiting for a formal request
- Being willing to share the limelight with other members when the team is successful
- Helping members to get to know and feel comfortable with each other
- Using humor and discussions of subjects other than work to relieve tension and smooth over awkward moments

Participation

In an effective team, everyone participates. Although in effective teams all team members will actively participate, participation will vary; that is, not everyone will participate equally or in the same manner. In the course of a team building exercise, I have observed and charted the participation levels of many teams. As a result, I am a firm believer in the theory of *weighted participation*. According to this concept, it is the quality and, more important, the *impact* of the participation that must be calculated. Although clearly this is a subjective measurement (as opposed to the simple counting of the number of times a team member speaks), a trained observer can easily make a judgment about contributions.

I observed one business team for many years, and one member comes to mind who reflects weighted participation in its purest sense. Jack is "economical" in his communication. He speaks only four or five times in a two-hour meeting. He wastes few words, gets to the point, and does not repeat himself. Jack's participation usually has impact because he provides useful information the team needs at the time; summarizes the key points, conclusions, or tentative decisions; or simply points out how the group has been wasting time and needs to move on. His primary style is challenger (see Chapter Three).

Other team members participate extensively but not always in the verbal discussions. You can tell they are involved because they participate nonverbally by nodding, leaning forward, and taking notes. Some team members will prepare reports, handouts, and presentations; others will set up the meeting room, get the necessary equipment, or arrange for an outside expert to attend the meeting.

The type of participation may vary, and it is important to measure both the manner and impact to determine if your team meets the test of extensive participation. The objective of effective participation is to encourage all team members to participate. Another key participation indicator, therefore, is *opportunity*. Effective teams provide all members with an opportunity to participate. Conversely, we have all known teams in which a few people dominated the action and limited the participation of other team members. It is the role of the team leader or meeting facilitator to help establish the climate, including appropriate ground rules that encourage quiet members to join the discussion and dissuade very talkative members from dominating the conversation.

At the same time, it is important to understand that members of cross-functional teams often feel they are permitted to comment only on issues within their area of expertise. For example, the engineer assumes that he should not participate in the consideration of the marketing plan. However, his knowledge of the inner workings of the product may help fashion a marketing strategy that may bring a very practical point of view to the plan. Again, the team needs ground rules and meeting facilitation that encourage participation by all members, regardless of their discipline and formal training.

In a similar vein, cultural differences can have a significant impact on the nature and degree of participation. If all business meetings in the organization are conducted in English, many members for whom English is not their primary language may experience difficulty in actively participating in team discussions. If Americans and others speak fast or use slang, other team members may not fully understand the message and will therefore be reluctant to join the conversation. In addition, people from some cultures may find it uncomfortable to speak in large groups or may feel that they should wait to be asked before providing information or giving their opinion. On the other hand, lack of participation by members can often be misunderstood and may sometimes be taken as a lack of interest. For example, in one study of cross-cultural virtual teams, "some participants expressed frustration at other team members who did not speak during telephone conferences, but other participants suggested that they would prefer someone to invite them to speak (rather than interrupt) during team conversations" (Anawati and Craig, 2006). The message: meeting facilitation may require (1) calling on people rather than waiting for them to offer comments and (2) adding a ground rule that encourages members (not just the leader) to solicit comments from their teammates.

In the new world of teams, with so many meetings held via teleconference, the requirement of effective participation becomes a greater challenge for global teams. The nonverbal cues that a facilitator may pick up in a face-to-face meeting are just not available. Therefore, in a teleconference and sometimes in a video conference as well (when the video feed is less than clear), the team leader as well as team members must be alert to the need to ensure that everyone in the meeting is given the opportunity to contribute their ideas. Again, as much as we try to avoid using direct questions, good teleconference facilitation may require that the leader simply call on nonparticipating members with an encouraging comment to get them engaged in the discussion:

- "Greta, you have a lot of experience in this area; what do you think of the proposal?"
- "Jonathan, with your background in packaging, I would very much like to hear your views."

Many facilitators of teleconferences are now asking for a response from everyone on the line before a decision is recorded because they want to be sure that everyone is on board before the meeting ends and the decision is placed in the minutes. The leader simply calls everyone by name or asks for responses by location ("Let's hear from the folks in London on this issue"). If the team is using the consensus method for decision making, the leader wants to ensure that everyone has a chance to express their opinion and that, in the end, all support (or can "live with") the proposed outcome. (See a later discussion in this chapter for more on consensus decision making.)

Participation should be relevant to the goal or task of the team. Teams often engage in a great deal of talk, but much of it is off the mark. I have worked with a number of teams in which there was a great deal of good-natured kidding, storytelling, and discussions of members' personal lives. The members genuinely enjoyed each other and looked forward to the interaction that accompanied team meetings. Unfortunately, very little work was accomplished, few decisions were reached, and progress toward goals was minimal. And my interventions, which were directed toward making the discussions more task-relevant, were met with strong objections. They resented my implication that they are not an effective team. "We're communicating, aren't we?" was a typical team-member response. Beneath the surface was the belief that any changes in the team would destroy the delicate balance that was keeping the group from coming apart. Often, there were deep divisions that were being covered by the humor and trivial discussions.

Dealing with participation that is not relevant to the meeting purpose can be tricky. We want an informal, relaxed climate, but it must be combined with a focus on goals and tasks at hand. My approach has been to get the team to address their degree of satisfaction with accomplishments or progress toward goals. Interviews, surveys, or guided group discussions are simple but effective techniques for collecting data about participation and its relationship to team effectiveness. In a recent data collection activity at a major corporation, the biggest complaint about team meetings was the failure to "stay on track." Although good facilitation skills are important, they can work only when there is a "track." The track is the key meeting outcome and a very specific agenda. With these tools in hand, the facilitator can intervene to note discussions that are not relevant and suggest that the team return to the agenda or refocus on the key meeting outcome; for example:

- "We seem to have drifted from our original agenda topic. Can we return to our discussion of the problems with the vendor?"
- "Although this discussion is obviously important to some of you, we still need to get back to our key meeting outcome, which is to come up with a plan to address the decrease in the customer satisfaction index. I suggest that we put this current issue in the 'parking lot' and add it to the agenda of our next meeting."

What to Do with the Chronic Nonparticipator

Despite the fact that psychological studies continually show the value of involvement by all team members, some people just do not want to participate. By the way, participation in a group is shown to also contribute to personal satisfaction as much as the participation helps the group succeed. Nevertheless, we find a small minority of team members who do not enjoy the group experience and prefer to work—and be—alone. For these people, their manager may simply not require that they join a team but rather allow them to make their contribution by providing needed assistance directly to the team without serving as a team member and attending team meetings.

In some other cases, a team may need the expertise of the "talented loner" (Straub, 1997) and, specifically, the opportunity for members of the team to engage in a discussion with this person. In this situation, the team leader or her manager should have a meeting with the "loner" to explain the importance of this interaction for the team and, ultimately, the organization. The manager might include participation in the team as part of her development plan and recommend some corporate training programs that may help the person.

There is another approach that has worked, especially in small to medium-size organizations, where there are limited functional resources. For example, one company had only two people in the strategic sourcing area and many more teams that needed the expertise of people with experience in dealing with vendors. In this situation, they elected to make the sourcing experts available on an as-needed basis whereby they would attend team meetings only when this topic was discussed. Alternatively, some teams elected to have a member of the team go to the sourcing person, get the necessary information, and bring it back to the team.

Other companies have instituted the shared services model. In this approach, certain services—such as human resources, legal, and purchasing—work in a centralized, corporate-wide department. Business units that need their expertise come to them on a project basis.

Participation can be enhanced by team players who

- Limit their participation to the agenda item under consideration
- Intervene when the participation is not relevant to the task
- Encourage silent members to participate in the discussion
- Speak out even when their views are contrary to the majority

Listening

The single most important factor distinguishing effective teams from ineffective ones is the ability of team members to listen to each other. It is a skill that serves as an underpinning for all the other determinants of effectiveness. Sadly, this is one area that gets more lip service than action. Although everyone agrees that listening skills are important, little is done to develop that capacity in team members.

I am intrigued by the popularity of workshops in memory development, business writing, speed reading, and public speaking, and by the contrasting lack of interest in listening-skills seminars. The assumption is, I suspect, that if your auditory system is functioning, you are able to listen effectively.

There are four communication skills: (1) reading, (2) writing, (3) speaking, and (4) listening. This list presents the four skills in an order based on the amount of time the average person spends in training to develop the skill. Unfortunately, this list is an inverse ranking of the degree to which adults need to use the skills in the business world. In other words, listening and speaking are more widely used and more valuable capabilities than are writing and reading. Therefore, we have the problematic and unfortunate situation of the communication skills that are in greatest demand receiving the least resources for training and development.

The principal listening skill is the ability to sit back, be attentive, and take in what is said while reserving judgment. We can absorb and process words spoken by other people much faster than they can verbalize the information. This leaves us lots of time to analyze, evaluate, and even anticipate the thoughts of the speaker. But this extra time can be a disadvantage, as we tend to concentrate minimally on what is being said and often discount comments before they are completed. The ability to listen *and reserve judgment* is critical if the ideas of teammates are to be given adequate consideration. This skill is especially important for team problem solving and decision making.

Another important listening skill is the capacity for *active listening*. Active listening takes a variety of forms. In its most basic and perhaps most powerful manifestation, team members react nonverbally to the contributions of others by nodding, maintaining eye contact, and leaning forward. They may add short verbal acknowledgments such as "I see" and "Uh-huh." Active listening is all the more powerful because it so rarely happens. Therefore, when someone really listens, you are doubly impressed—with yourself and with the other person. The person is saying "I'm interested in what you have to say."

A sometimes more powerful active listening skill is paraphrasing facts and feelings. Sometimes called *reflecting*, the classic response begins, "What I hear you saying is . . ." Or "You seem upset about . . ." The goal of paraphrasing or reflecting is (1) to make sure you are clear about what is intended by the other team member and (2) to let the other person know you care about what he or she is communicating.

We have all had the experience of using words that we knew were not really communicating to other team members what we were feeling or thinking. The techniques of active listening are strong tools for helping all team members find the right words to express their thoughts or feelings and to maximize their contributions to the team effort.

In another sense, active listening helps team players develop self-understanding. In the process of explaining their thoughts, the team members often come to a better understanding of the

Table 2.2 Active Listening

Use of Active Listening	Examples
1. To convey interest in what the other person is saying	I see!
2. To encourage the individual to expand further on his or her thinking	Yes, go on. Tell us more.
3. To help the individual clarify the problem in his or her own thinking	Then the problem as you see it is . . .
4. To get the individual to hear what he or she has said in the way it sounded to others	This is your decision then, and the reasons are . . . If I understand you correctly, you are saying that we should . . .
5. To pull out the key ideas from a long statement or discussion	Your major point is . . . You feel that we should . . .
6. To respond to a person's feeling more than to his or her words	You feel strongly that . . . You do not believe that . . .
7. To summarize specific points of agreement and disagreement as a basis for further discussion	We seem to be agreed on the following points . . . but we seem to need further clarification on these points . . .
8. To express a consensus of group feeling	As a result of this discussion, we as a group seem to feel that . . .

issue. In short, we are providing them with a chance to alter their thoughts and feelings. Table 2.2 provides some examples of the uses of active listening.

Although active listening is a key skill for member-to-member communication, it is also very important for the team leader. As a key facilitation skill, the leader uses active listening to

- Encourage members to participate, because when someone really listens to you, it is a strong motivator to increase your participation
- Ensure that important facts, data, and other information are understood by all members so an informed decision can be made
- Resolve differences among members by ensuring that the real issues are discussed, unclouded by the emotions
- Summarize discussions so the team can stay on track and effectively manage team meeting time
- Clarify proposed conclusions or other team actions so that members are clear about what is being decided

In the new world of cross-functional and cross-cultural teams, active listening remains an important success factor. In a cross-functional team, the marketing professional has to understand the issues presented to the team by the clinical trial leader. The challenge of achieving clear communication across disciplines is often made more difficult when the two people are culturally different. One important method for dealing with these challenges is to use the skill of paraphrasing or reflecting. In a recent study of 122 cross-cultural virtual team members, "participants identified repeating themselves using different words as a way to increase the chance of team members understanding" (Anawati and Craig, 2006, p. 50).

Similarly, with the members of many of these cross-cultural teams geographically dispersed around the world, teleconferencing has become the most widely used meeting method. As noted in the previous section, achieving widespread participation by members during a teleconference is difficult under the best of circumstances, but when you add cross-functional and cross-cultural diversity, the challenge becomes even more daunting. Encouraging paraphrasing by members in these meetings is very important. However, it is even more important that the team leader have high-level active listening skills in his or her repertoire and use them often. In our meeting facilitation skills workshops, we spend more time on this topic than on any of the other fifteen facilitator behaviors!

Team players can support the norm of high-level listening by

- Reserving judgment on a presentation until all the data are presented and analyzed
- Being willing to learn and act on opinions and facts that may alter the team mission or goals
- Modeling the effective listening skills (for example, paraphrasing) for other team members
- Summarizing differences and acknowledging when their views differ from those of other team members

Civilized Disagreement

Disagreement is, of course, a euphemism for conflict. We tend to shy away from the word *conflict* because it connotes negative behavior or, at the very least, an unpleasant relationship. We have developed many of our feelings about the word because of media headlines such as "Middle East Conflict," "Labor-Management Conflict," and "Conflict Between City Hall and the Gay Community." Therefore, conflict is portrayed as war and thus is a situation to be avoided. In terms of effective teamwork, nothing could be further from the truth.

Conflicts will occur especially in the new world of cross-cultural, cross-functional virtual teams (Baba, Gluesing, Ratner, and Wagner, 2004; Anawati and Craig, 2006). For example, members representing different functions come to the team with different work orientations. Members from operations tend to be short-term and task-oriented, whereas research and development people are likely to have a long-range view with no great sense of immediacy. Software developers are more inclined to focus internally on the quality of the product, whereas the sales staff looks externally at the impact on the willingness of the customer to purchase the product. The team needs to consider all these orientations, but until they develop the ability to address them in a constructive manner, harmful conflict will result.

Conflicts can arise on a cross-cultural, global team when there are different modes of work vying for supremacy. In one study of a global team dominated by French and American members, it was pointed out that "the French tend to rely on long-term, personal relationships and networks for the conduct of daily business and generally respect the organizational hierarchy for the purposes of communication and coordination [whereas, by contrast, Americans] . . . tend to be action-oriented and thus focused pragmatically on getting the job done; the organizational hierarchy may be more or less salient . . ." (Baba and others, 2004, p. 560). Problems arise when these conflicts are not resolved satisfactorily because many teams have not learned the requisite conflict-resolution skills. Communication, knowledge sharing, decision making, and many other skills critical to success will be flawed.

In the new reality of team players and teamwork, these potential emerging conflicts create more demands on the team leader. It is more difficult and requires more sophisticated skills to resolve the differences that members bring to the team that have little to do with the work but may have a major impact on the success of the team. In addition, with management's expectations for team success at a much higher level, there is little patience for these conflicts. Management presumes these differences will be resolved quickly and the team will get focused on the "real" work.

Disagreements about the work of the team should be encouraged and accepted as a natural consequence of a dynamic, active team. Effective teams create a climate in which people feel free to express their opinions even when those opinions are at odds with those of other team members. We encourage all teams to establish norms or ground rules that support the free expression of differences.

Problems often arise from the manner in which an opinion is expressed. Attacking another team member, denigrating the opposite position, a hostile tone or voice, or an aggressive hand gesture can lead to destructive conflict. In short, we get *uncivilized disagreement*. Clearly, as indicated in Table 2.3, conflict can be either destructive or constructive.

Effective teams want differences to be expressed; members use their communication and listening skills to ensure that all points surface. They see diversity as a strength of the team. As a result, team members are supported in their efforts to articulate their

Table 2.3 Aspects of Conflict

Destructive	*Constructive*
Diverts energy from more important activities and issues	Opens up issues of importance, resulting in their clarification
Destroys the morale of people or reinforces poor self-concept	Leads to the solution of problems
Polarizes groups so they increase internal cohesiveness and reduce intergroup cooperation	Increases the involvement of individuals in issues of importance to them
Deepens differences in values	Causes authentic communication to occur
Produces irresponsible and regrettable behavior such as name-calling and fighting	Serves as a release for pent-up emotion, anxiety, and stress
	Helps build cohesion among people sharing the conflict, celebrating in its settlement, and learning more about each other
	Helps individuals grow personally and apply what they learn to future situations

Source: Adapted from Hart, 1980, p. 6.

ideas, to come forth with contrary information, and to discuss their feelings in a positive manner. (One company recently had a division-wide initiative to encourage all members to "speak up" because management felt this was so important to corporate success.)

Unfortunately, because conflict continues to be a dirty word, differences often linger unexpressed, leading the parties to become contentious, and outcomes are arrived at in such a manner that no one feels satisfied.

I have encountered five different methods of resolving conflicts: *denial, smoothing over, power, compromise,* and *problem solving.*

When *denial* is operating, team members simply do not recognize or, more accurately, do not acknowledge the existence of any dissension. They simply go about their business, often going on to the next agenda item without the blink of an eye. If someone on the team asks about the "problem," other team members will refer to the matter as a "healthy discussion" or "good exchange of ideas" and then move on.

Smoothing over is the first cousin of denial, although here the conflict or difference of opinion is admitted but characterized as "trivial." Team members are advised not to worry about it, but, of course, everybody secretly wishes that it would go away. There is a strong feeling among some people that talking about problems, feelings, and conflicts only makes them worse. A favorite ploy to smother conflict is the use of humor. Tension among colleagues may make other team members uncomfortable, and joking relieves the tension. But this can lead to avoidance of any serious consideration of the issues. Humor is important to the success of a team, but in excess it can detract from the group's mission, and when misused it can deter discussion of important problems.

The third method of resolving conflicts is use of *power.* The simplest, cleanest, and easiest way is for one person to decide the outcome. One team member may be the boss or may in some other way have control over the behavior of the others. Therefore, when conflicts arise, members of the team turn to this person for "the word." In a more subtle version of the power game, team members discuss their differences, and it may appear that some real team problem solving is taking place. Then, when a deadline approaches or the meeting is about to end, the "power" person steps in with a decision to "save time" or "move along."

Compromise is the most deceptive and seductive method of conflict resolution. Like cotton candy, it looks good on the outside, but when you are finished, it is not very satisfying. Compromise, in its crudest form, is "splitting the differences." Say you believe the team should meet six times a year whereas I think four meetings are sufficient. After some discussion, we settle on five meetings, and on the surface this decision looks great. However, neither of us is satisfied; we have just minimized our dissatisfaction. More important, we have not worked toward a decision that is best for our team; rather, we have worked toward a decision that is acceptable. Compromise is used when team members want to reduce the extent of the conflict and avoid the work associated with problem solving.

Problem solving, sometimes called collaborative conflict resolution, is the most difficult but potentially the most satisfying method. This approach requires that team members acknowledge that some differences exist, agree to deal with the issues and not smooth them over, forgo power as a quick and easy alternative, and avoid simple compromises when the problems are complex and important.

Effective problem solving begins with a discussion leading ultimately to an agreement on a problem statement. This discussion may involve an examination of where we are now versus where we want to be. In other contexts, we talk about degree of nonconformance, plan versus actual, or current condition against standard. Sometimes the development of a problem statement involves constructing the ideal or desired state, as in "How would it look if there were no communications problems?"

The next step is problem analysis. This is when we want the participation of team members who have data and opinions. Research and study by team members may also be necessary.

Generating alternative solutions is an important step that is often overlooked. Too often, teams jump to the first available answer without considering other possibilities. Few problems have only one possible solution. Solution selection should involve as many team members as possible. Although the team needs a diversity of ideas, the team's commitment to the ultimate solution is equally important. Participation in the decision-making process will help ensure the team's support for the implementation of the solution.

This collaborative approach to conflict resolution moves a team toward a search for the best response to a problem. Successful application of this method also leads to strengthening of the team and increases group cohesion. Team players can establish a climate for civilized disagreement by

- Maintaining an objective, analytical approach to the differences
- Being flexible and open to all points of view
- Defusing overt hostility through the use of humor
- Backing off when their views are not being accepted by the rest of the team

Consensus

A centerpiece of the effective team is the use of the consensus method for making key decisions. A consensus requires unity, but not unanimity; concurrence, but not consistency. The problem-solving approach to conflict resolution implies differences among team members, and consensus is the technique to reach agreement about the problem statement and the recommended solution. Here is how it works:

A consensus is reached when all members can say they either agree with the decision or have had their "day in court" and were unable to convince the others of their viewpoint. In the final analysis, everyone agrees to support the outcome. It is not a majority, because that implies a vote, and voting is *verboten* for teams using the consensus method. Voting tends to split the group into winners and losers, thereby creating needless divisions. Consensus does not require unanimity, because members may still disagree with the final result but are willing to work toward its success. This is the hallmark of a team player. Table 2.4 provides some tips for successful use of the consensus method.[3]

In a steering committee meeting, the group had to decide on the format for an upcoming company conference. Bruce argued strongly for an overnight session because it would allow sufficient social time after the meetings to facilitate informal get-togethers, which he felt were important for improving intergroup communication. The other committee members agreed with the need for the social aspect but felt the lodging costs would not be viewed positively by upper management. As an alternative, they proposed a one-day conference ending at 4:00 P.M. followed by a two-hour cocktail party. Bruce still felt the overnight was preferable but went along with the one-day alternative as "the best approach, given the current cost-containment environment." A consensus had been reached.

Table 2.4 Using the Consensus Method

Do's	Don'ts
Use active listening skills	Horse-trade
Involve as many members as possible	Vote
Seek out the reasons behind arguments; dig for the facts	Agree, just to avoid "rocking the boat"

Horse-trading is a variation of the compromise approach to conflict resolution. It means that I got something that was important to me on the last round, so this time I will go along with your pet project. To get the best decisions, teams must avoid even subtle horse-trading.

One of the major arguments against the consensus method is that it is too time-consuming. It is true that it takes longer than the autocratic (one person decides) and democratic (majority vote) systems. However, autocratic and democratic decisions often unravel because the team does not truly support the outcome, so members are unwilling to put forth the effort required for successful implementation.

I remember a workshop participant once telling me, "Glenn, this consensus approach is fine. But I just do not want a pilot on my next flight having a nice group discussion with the crew when the plane is having engine problems and in danger of crashing. I want one person in charge."

This sounds right, but research and practice in the airline industry clearly indicate the need for more teamwork in the cockpit. There are few situations in which a split-second decision is required. In most cases, time *is* available to collect data, share ideas, and make a decision. The statistics on the causes of fatal accidents and near misses are so powerful that several airlines have taken action to develop cockpit management skills and to improve teamwork among airline personnel. The now infamous Eastern Airline flight 401, which crashed near Miami in 1972 killing some 150 people, is used as a case study of poor team management. To avoid such situations, pilots are now taught participative management skills and other crew members learn how to be more assertive.

The consensus approach has its place even in difficult situations, but it is not always appropriate. It must be used judiciously. Your team should use the consensus technique when

- There is no clear answer
- There is no single expert in the group

- Commitment to the decision is essential
- Sufficient time is available
- And, most important, the decision is worthy of the time and effort required to reach a true consensus

In the new team environment, it is important to be on the alert for the so-called "False-Positive Consensus" (Parker, 2002, p. 348). Sometimes a team leader thinks a consensus has been reached because no verbal objections are expressed, as in the following fictitious scenario:

"Janet has proposed that we go with ECC as our vendor for the environmental studies on this project. How do the rest of you feel about it? What questions do you have for Janet about the vendor or the contract? It seems as though all of the questions and concerns have been addressed and that there are no objections to the decision to contract with ECC for the work. Unless I hear any comments to the contrary, I am going to assume that we have reached a consensus on this issue. Let's move on to our next agenda item."

This type of consensus can be treacherous for the team and the organization, since it is likely to cause problems in the future. I have worked with teams that frequently revisited decisions, causing negative feelings among members, a waste of valuable time, delay in completing projects, and a misuse of company resources. As noted in previous sections of this chapter, some team members are reluctant to speak up in meetings, to disagree with colleagues, or ask what they mistakenly think are "stupid" questions. A False-Positive Consensus can arise when

- People from some cultures (such as Japan) are reluctant to publicly disagree with teammates (Oertig and Buergi, 2006)
- Members from different functions do not believe they are supposed to comment on topics outside their area of expertise

or, similarly, do not have the confidence to ask a question about the work of a colleague from another functional area

- Assumed pressure from management to complete the project quickly leads members to refrain from questioning a decision for fear of wasting time
- The leader lacks the facilitation skills to get participation from members, "read" the group's feeling about a proposed decision, or listen actively to the responses of members
- A critical decision must be made during a teleconference and the type of active involvement necessary for reaching a solid consensus is very difficult, even for an effective team with a skilled facilitator

Consensus decisions can be facilitated by team players who

- Press for reasons and data to support decisions
- Discourage the use of other decision-making tactics (for example, voting and one-person rule)
- Periodically summarize and test possible decisions with the group
- Are willing to go along with the team's consensus even though they may disagree with it
- During a teleconference, will insist that everyone on the line be polled to ensure that all opinions are included

Open Communication and Trust

A company president complained to me that all his management board meetings were too cheerful. "Everyone is so polite to each other," he remarked. Conflicts existed among the vice presidents but were never addressed. There was a low level of trust among the group members, resulting in reluctance to discuss key issues openly. Individual vice presidents talked to the president about their problems with other VPs and hoped the president would handle them (meaning that he would talk to the other person).

"Trust implies that people will keep their promises, speak truthfully, keep their word and act morally. Trust assumes that people share common value. *Trust is fragile* because it is always subject to betrayal" (Kahane, 2006, p. 52, emphasis added).

Trust is clearly the avenue to open communication. Members must have confidence that they can reveal aspects of themselves and their work without fear of reprisals or embarrassment. The higher the level of trust, the more risks team members are willing to take.

When a new team forms, typically the level of trust among all members is low. They are defensive and interact with each other from their formal role positions. They are testing each other, forming norms of acceptable behavior, with the goal of safety in interpersonal relations. The formal leader tends to be more controlling, as he or she exercises considerable leadership authority.

Initially, the flow of communication is distorted as team members "play their cards close to the vest." As the team matures, trust increases, with a corresponding increase in openness, in confrontation of issues, and in the use of influence skills. At the outset, goal setting and planning are often competitive activities as team members are intent on winning a game of wits. Later, as they are able to be honest with each other, the team adopts a problem-solving mode in which members are open to learning from each other. In one study of project teams, "interviewees estimated a range of three to nine months as the time needed to develop a comfort level and trust level with new members" (Oertig and Buergi, 2006, p. 26). (Chapter Six includes a comprehensive discussion of the stages of team development.)

Open communication and trust typically develop over time and with experience in working with colleagues on a team. Over time, it becomes clear that their teammates will

- Make only commitments they expect to keep
- Honor their commitments on a consistent basis

- Provide honest assessments, including problems and obstacles
- Take responsibility for their actions, including mistakes and delays
- Maintain confidentiality, as required and expected

On global virtual teams, it is clearly more difficult to develop trust quickly because team members have limited opportunity to interact on a face-to-face basis. In addition, cultural differences can make trust-building more challenging when some team members come with culture-based values about open communication, especially discussing problems in public and admitting mistakes to others. Lack of trust can therefore inhibit rapid team development and so create tension, especially when senior management is expecting results in a timely fashion. However, "when trust thrives in an organization (and a team), good things happen—people cooperate, share expertise, tell the truth, work harder and listen to each other. Employees work hard for the organization (and team) because they see themselves as valued members of a team and as stakeholders" (Kahane, 2006, p. 52).

As a result, more recently, there is a movement toward the concept of "swift trust" (Myerson, Weick, and Kramer, 1996). In response to the demands for more rapid team development and the production of results, team members are encouraged to assume all members of the team are trustworthy from the outset. If you assume that the other person can be trusted, there is no need for all those little "tests" to occur over time and with experience. In other words, the attitude becomes "I trust that you will honor your commitments" rather than "I will know I can trust you if and when you honor your commitments."

Team players can encourage open communication and trust by

- Being dependable and trustworthy—someone on whom the team can rely to deliver on commitments, tell the truth, and admit mistakes
- Pitching in and helping other team members who need assistance

- Reading and responding to nonverbal cues that suggest a lack of openness
- Candidly sharing views and encouraging others to do the same

The leader's behavior is crucial in building trust and opening communication. First, the leader must encourage discussion of problems and key issues and then model a response that is nonjudgmental. It must be seen as OK to ask for help or to seek the advice of other team members. Second, the leader should support (and feel comfortable with) the concept of subgroups of team members working together. This "decontrolling" is critical for group growth. Third, the leader has to be trusting and trustworthy. The leader must empower members to take responsibility for certain tasks without checking on them constantly. The leader also has to provide accurate and complete information to the team, honor commitments to the members, and be willing to take responsibility for errors in judgment. Finally, the leader has to be an expert in cultural values that may have an impact on trust and open communication in order to advise on how to use these differences to build a more effective team. However, a major study of global teams reported that "knowledge of the generally acceptable behavior of members of a culture is only a departure point for a global leader. She/he has to get to know the individual member in order to understand how their behavior may be informed by the national cultural pressures even though their actual behavior may ultimately be different" (Barczak, McDonough, and Athanassiou, 2006, p. 32).

Clear Roles and Work Assignments

Every team member has a formal job with a series of functions often defined in a job description or specification. The concept of *role* goes beyond a listing of tasks to the expectations a specific team member has about his or her job and to the expectations that other team members have about that job. Since effective teamwork involves task interdependence, agreement on these expectations is extremely important. The work of the team will not be optimized if team members do not know what others expect of them or if there is a conflict in expectations.

During interviews in preparation for team building with a group of health professionals, it became clear to me that role conflict was the problem. I asked all team members how they viewed the critical jobs on the team. In summarizing the interview data, it became clear that there were widely varying expectations of several of the key players. A number of techniques for clarifying expectations were available, but I elected to use a brief version of role negotiations (Harrison, 1971) in which each team member enlists the aid of other members in doing his or her job more effectively. These requests brought out some expectations that had not been communicated previously and some other expectations that were conflicting or difficult to implement. A process of clarification, exploring alternatives, and agreement culminated in a series of "contracts" among team members. In the final analysis, conflicts that were surfacing as personality differences turned out to be conflicts in role expectations.

Awareness of the importance of roles is essential to the success of a team. Teams often see conflicts among their members on the emotional (feelings) level when, in fact, the conflict is substantive (roles, procedures). Role conflict and ambiguity can cause considerable stress on the team and can result in lost productivity, dissatisfaction, and a tendency of members to leave the team.

Role clarification is important at any time. It is useful when (1) data collection reveals a diagnosis of role conflict or ambiguity, as in this case; (2) a new team is forming; or (3) a new member joins the team.

Role clarification has increased in importance in the new team environment.

- In a cross-functional team, members often lack clarity about what can be expected of members from other functions. For example, a member from engineering may not understand the role of marketing on a new product team or may have a distorted view of the marketing function. A similar lack of understanding may exist for the marketing person in regard to the role of engineering. Role confusion leads to unrealistic expectations and potential conflict.

- Cultural differences on global teams may result in role ambiguity. There are different views of role in different cultures. Americans, for example, tend to view role as something more clearly defined, with identified boundaries ("*This* is my job and *that* is your job"), whereas people in other cultures are more comfortable with what might be called "leaky margins" between roles that allow overlap in responsibilities.

- In regulated industries (such as pharmaceuticals and utilities), the team members who deal with government agencies often feel that their teammates do not appreciate the challenges they face in dealing with compliance requirements.

- Given the growing trend toward more geographically dispersed teams, it is now more important and, at the same time, more of a challenge for the team leader to understand the roles of members representing a wide variety of functions. "Clearly defined roles and responsibilities enable individual team members to know what their particular tasks are when dispersed and hold each accountable for those activities" (Barczak, McDonough, and Athanassiou, 2006, p. 33).

A great deal of teamwork takes place outside of team meetings. In order for teams to be effective, they must make clear-cut decisions and plan necessary follow-up actions.

In my experience, the most successful teams are those in which team members take responsibility for work assignments critical to the achievement of the team's mission. They volunteer for jobs such as collecting data, drafting reports, preparing presentations, and setting up meetings.

Assignments must also be completed on time. Effective team players are committed to the team, and as a result, they would not dare come unprepared to a meeting. In today's world the best teams have a norm that requires team members to send all reports, background materials, and other relevant information out to the team in advance of the next meeting. This procedure helps the team save time during the meetings and allows members to be prepared for team decisions.

One key test for team effectiveness is the extent to which task assignments are distributed among team members. The negative effects of a team in which a few people carry the major workload quickly become obvious. At first, things seem very efficient, and a great deal of work gets done. Soon, however, these people experience burnout or, worse, resentment toward other team members. Eventually, this kind of team deteriorates into a loose group with a small core of workers and others who are members in name only.

Members of effective teams never say, "That's not my job." When team members realize that one of their colleagues has an especially difficult or time-consuming assignment, they offer to help. One situation that illustrated this point was an assignment to locate an appropriate conference facility for an off-site company meeting. This assignment was difficult because of certain location, facilities, and budget constraints. One team member volunteered to conduct the basic research of contacting a number of potential conference centers and collecting information. She then turned over the information to the responsible team member, who used the data for analysis and subsequent negotiations.

Another team I know of does not allow team members to send substitutes to the meetings. This rule tends to ensure that all assignments are completed on time because team members cannot skip a meeting if they have not done their homework. However, in companies in which people may serve on many teams, this rule is modified to allow a member to send a "briefed" substitute. The team member is required to prepare the substitute by providing background on the issues to be discussed and copies of all relevant documents.

Effective role clarification and assignments occur when team players:

- Push the team to set high quality standards for work contributed by members
- Are willing to work outside their defined roles when necessary
- Ensure that assignments are evenly distributed among team members
- Openly discuss and negotiate their expectations of each team member's role

Shared Leadership

All teams have a formal leader. A variety of titles are used to designate the position: project manager, team leader, supervisor, coach, chairperson, coordinator, captain, director, or, simply, the boss. Traditionally, we give a great deal of authority and, accordingly, much responsibility to the leader for the success of the team. This is just plain wrong. Over the long haul, a team will not be successful if the leader carries the sole responsibility for ensuring that the team reaches its goals. Leadership of a team must be shared among team members. Everyone must feel and take responsibility for meeting the task and process needs of the team. If the team fails, everybody fails. This is one of the most important concepts of team effectiveness, but it is also the most difficult to teach.

Clearly, it is easier and, for many people, more desirable to have someone who will tell us what to do, when to do it, and how to do it. And it is convenient to have someone to blame! One of the most frustrating things for me is to leave a team meeting and meet a member in the hall who says, "Well, wasn't that a waste of time?" My response is always the same: "Don't bring it up to me after the meeting. This does no good at all. Next time, say something during the meeting when it counts. It is your team, your meeting, your valuable time, and, therefore, your responsibility to do whatever it takes (for example, ask the group to stick to the agenda) to help ensure it is not a waste of time."

In many situations, the formal leader is either unaware of or unable to exercise the required leadership function at the time it is needed. And I did use the word *leadership* to describe the activity. In its most basic form, leadership is any action that helps a team reach its goals. Members of successful teams use words such as *our* and *we* when referring to their teams.

In successful teams, leadership is shared. Although the formal leader has certain administrative, legal, and bureaucratic responsibilities, leadership functions shift from time to time among team members, depending on the needs of the group and the skills of the members. Behavioral scientists have categorized these functions as *task responsibilities* and *process responsibilities*.

As the name implies, *task responsibilities* are actions that help the team reach its goal, accomplish an immediate task, make a decision, or solve a problem. Teams tend to be most effective in this area because, by training and temperament, people are more task oriented. Most role models and most training in education and business settings focus on what to do to accomplish a task. Consider all the books and workshops on such topics as time management, meeting planning, and goal setting.

For *process responsibilities*, the emphasis is on how we go about accomplishing our task. It is the interpersonal glue that helps maintain or, better yet, exploit all our team's resources. On the whole, teams tend to be less process oriented because traditional training stresses such axioms as "The end justifies the means" and "Winning is everything." Effective teams, however, know that the quality of their decisions is impacted by the manner in which they make their judgments.

In the new team environment, in which many teams are cross-functional, cross-cultural, and virtual and are composed of people who are on multiple teams, effective leadership is now more of a necessity. Elsewhere I have said that leading a cross-functional team is the most difficult of all team leadership positions (Parker, 2003). Specifically, leading a cross-functional team involves the following:

- Leading by influence rather than authority, as all of the team members report to the manager of their function
- Dealing with the competing interests and conflicting priorities of members who may be serving on three or four other teams
- Negotiating with senior management for team resources in competition with other team leaders who believe their project is just as important
- Negotiating with functional managers to empower the representatives from their area who serve on the cross-functional team and to provide other resources needed by the project
- Coordinating the efforts of a diverse group of people who bring a wide variety of backgrounds, styles, and interest in your project
- Facilitating meetings conducted via teleconference, video conference, or web conference, with only a rare face-to-face meeting

The message in all of the above is that it is too much to expect that the leader, even a very good one, can do it alone. Successful teamwork in today's business environment must be, as the saying goes, "a team effort!" Although effective leadership is necessary for effective teamwork, it is not sufficient. Effective teamwork requires the coordinated effort of all team members, backed by strong management support from both the "top of the house" as well as line managers.

Team players can help establish the norm of shared leadership by ensuring that both the task and process functions are addressed by the team. Some examples are found in Table 2.5.

Table 2.5 Leadership Responsibilities

Task	*Process*
Initiating: proposing tasks, goals, or actions; defining group problems; suggesting a procedure	Harmonizing: attempting to reconcile disagreements; reducing tension; getting people to explore differences
Offering Facts: providing data and other information; giving an opinion	Gatekeeping: helping others to participate; keeping communication channels open; facilitating the participation of others
Seeking Information: asking for data, opinions, facts and feelings	
Clarifying: interpreting or elaborating ideas; asking questions in an effort to understand or promote understanding	Consensus Testing: asking if a group is nearing a decision; proposing a possible solution or decision that seems to be emerging from the group
Coordinating/Summarizing: pulling together related ideas; restating suggestions; offering a decision or conclusion for the group to consider	Encouraging: being friendly, warm, and responsive to others; indicating (by facial expression or remark) an interest in others' contributions
Reality Testing: making a critical analysis of an idea; testing an idea against some data; trying to see if the idea would work	Compromising: when one's own idea or status is involved in a conflict, offering a compromise that yields status; modifying in the interest of group cohesion or growth

External Relations

In *The Superteam Solution*, Hastings, Bixby, and Chaudhry-Lawton (1987) were the first to make us aware of the "importance of the invisible team"—customers, vendors, support groups, and sponsors. In certain regulated industries, invisible team members may also include government agency representatives. These other players make demands on the team, provide access to needed resources, and are a source of valuable feedback on team performance. As a point of clarification, it is important to understand that many of these people will not show up on the official roster of team names. However, the impact of these stakeholders on team success is great—in some cases they can be more important than any official team member (Parker, 2003; Ancona and Caldwell, 1992).

The resources of customers and clients are important indicators of success. Tom Peters has provided many examples of companies that regularly ask customers, "How are we doing?" (Peters, 1987). In the data processing field, there are many user groups and joint developer-user teams. "In today's complex and virtual organizations, managers (and team leaders) need information and support from a wide range of individuals. This is confirmed by research that shows a direct link between networking and effectiveness. The challenge is that building networks is a time-consuming activity. Its payoff comes in the long run. Most managers (and team leaders) focus on accomplishing tasks rather than building relationships; but in today's world they must do both well" (Conger and Lawler, 2005, p. 10).

Teams usually need a sponsor who can serve as a mentor and advocate: a good sponsor can increase the life of a team and provide access to needed resources (budget, staff, publicity).

Cross-functional teams need the cooperation of the functional departments from which team members are drawn. The managers of the functional departments can support the team by encouraging their people to give all assignments a high priority. In addition, service departments can provide information, staff, expertise, facilities, and equipment that can be vital to the success of the team.

The effective team builds key relationships with people outside the team. The team leader is usually the person with the responsibility for external relations, but the leader may not always be the best person to handle every contact. Even the person from the same discipline or with the requisite expertise may not be the most appropriate to handle the interface. Managing the "boundary" is an important aspect of teamwork, and selecting the best person is the key decision. For example, teams may elect to have a person who lacks the technical expertise but who possesses high-level negotiating skills to manage the budget process and one with good communications skills to facilitate a users' meeting.

Managing the "outside" often involves the creation of a positive image. Teams find that doing a good job is not enough; they must find ways to communicate their successes to significant others on the invisible team. Many teams create a newsletter, others resort to presentations at meetings, and still others focus on personal contact by team members. Lack of information about the team can lead to a lack of credibility. Ultimately, poor image can hamper success.

External relations also involve building a network of contacts who can assist the team. This network can help the team get an approval moved quickly through the bureaucracy, obtain funds for a special project, locate an expert to solve a team problem, smooth out a conflict with another organization, or find new product and service ideas.

All of this network building is geared to the mobilization of resources. Teams need help, and the effective teams get the resources they need when they need them. Effective teams lay the groundwork by building a positive image, confidence, and active support for their efforts. For global, new product teams, "creating new products with competitive advantage not only requires using the firm's own multinational resources and knowledge, but also the resources and knowledge of other companies and organizations, universities, vendors and even competitors. Commercialization of new product efforts is also no longer a local affair. Manufacturing, service, and sales often take place on different continents with staff from multiple countries. Successful leadership of global teams thus demands leaders who are able to develop and leverage networks and build

and maintain social capital" (Barczak, McDonough, and Athanassiou, 2006, p. 34).

Building support for a team is especially crucial for a new team
or for a team with a new idea. It is important for members to be
"engaged in a process of informing others, understanding and over-
coming their objections, understanding the factions and motives
of the different parties involved, lobbying and persuading these
key figures how the idea can benefit the organization" (Hastings,
Bixby, and Chaudhry-Lawton, 1987, p. 49).

The result of this networking can be some fascinating interpersonal dynamics. Effective teams are often seen as a "pain in
the butt." The use of this phrase implies both good-natured kidding and healthy respect. Sponsors, customers, and others would
sometimes just as soon avoid dealing with the team but are often
impressed with the team's fervor and tenacity.

Effective image building with the invisible team also has a
salutary effect on team members. As Hastings and his associates
(p. 50) note, "[effective] publicity breeds pride and pride reinforces
commitment."

Team players help the team build effective external relations by

- Completing all work assignments in their functional
  department
- Sharing the credit for team successes with members of the
  invisible team
- Informing members of the invisible team of important actions
  that may impact their interactions with the team
- Encouraging honest feedback from clients, customers, and
  sponsors

Style Diversity

Most of the thinking and writing about teamwork has focused
on the group dynamics of an effective team and on management
and leadership skills. Very little attention has been given to the

composition of the team as a determinant of success or to the concept of *team player*.

My research indicates a variety of ways in which a person can contribute to a team's success. The next chapter will present a detailed description of the various team player styles—indications of the many ways that members can be helpful to their team. Equally important is the finding that the most successful teams are composed of members who exhibit a diversity of styles. This finding means that a team increases its chances for success if it includes a mix of members who are concerned about high-quality task accomplishment, push the team to set goals and objectives, work hard to ensure a positive team process, and raise questions about the team's operations.

The team of health professionals with the role conflicts we discussed earlier in this chapter also had a diversity of team player styles. The team consisted of four people. When they completed the *Parker Team Player Survey* (see Resource C), the results revealed that each member's primary style was different from those of the other team members. In effect, the team had a "perfect" distribution of the styles—four members, four different styles. The team was composed of one task-focused member, one goal-directed member, one process-oriented member, and one member who questioned the team's methods. When the results were shared, team members recognized two things: (1) how the style differences had reinforced the role conflicts and (2) how the style differences strengthened the team.

We have seen the effects of teams without style diversity. For example, one team of systems developers seemed very busy. In fact, they did work very hard, spending long hours and weekends on their project. They were very bright and set high standards for their work, and they expected high quality from their colleagues. But then, at a project meeting, the frustration that had been building surfaced in an avalanche of self-criticism:

- "We've lost sight of the big picture."
- "This isn't fun anymore."

- "I'm not sure we're doing things right."
- "Are we all in agreement on where we want to be by the end of the year?"

With some help, they began to see their team as being task oriented to the exclusion of other styles. Members of the team were encouraged to expand their repertoire (1) to emphasize the big picture—specifically, to focus on where the project was going and where it fit into other organization efforts in the systems area; (2) to take the time to address the process needs of the team—specifically, to emphasize interpersonal relationships among team members; and (3) regularly to take a hard look at project outcomes and team effectiveness.

By the way, it is quite easy and almost natural for teams to be composed of members with similar orientations. When a team is being organized or when new members are added to an existing team, we look for variety in knowledge and skills to match the team's function. However, when it comes to deciding which engineer or computer programmer we will select, we look for similarity, not diversity. We look for "someone who will fit in," "my kind of guy," "a person who thinks the way we do," or "someone I can relate to."

People simply feel more comfortable around other people with similar styles. It takes an effort to appreciate another person with a different way of getting things done. Yet we know that diversity in both substance and style strengthens a team. Chapter Seven provides guidelines for analyzing your team's strengths and weaknesses and for developing strategies for improvement.

As teams have come to function in the new environment of global teams, the concept of diversity must be broadened to include both cultural and functional diversity. Culture and function both enrich and challenge the concept of team player style. We know, for example, that research and development folks tend to take a long-range view of their work; operations people are more inclined to be focused on the short-term goals and immediate tasks. Human resource professionals emphasize positive working relationships; scientists and technicians often ask the tough questions and challenge proposed solutions. Successful teams need all of these styles in an effort to look at all sides of an issue.

Culture also has an impact on style differences. Some cultures value direct and open communication, whereas others tend to build informal, social relationships as a prelude to decision-making. Some cultures respect hierarchical structures, whereas people from other cultures feel free to communicate with anyone regardless of their position in the organizational structure. Openly challenging the work of a colleague in a meeting would be considered disrespectful in some cultures; doing the same thing in another culture would be considered simply good business practice.

In the new world of teams, we can expect team members to bring a variety of styles to their current team. Each person's style will be based to a considerable extent on their personality but also, to some extent, on the degree to which they are influenced by their culture and function. In the end, team success depends on a diversity of styles, with each style bringing important strengths to the team. In today's complex world, teams need a variety of approaches to meet the important challenges. Successful teams know that although style diversity is important, it is the ability of team members to appreciate and use this diversity that is the critical factor in creating and sustaining a high-performing team.

Self-Assessment

Periodically, teams should stop to examine how well they are functioning and what may be interfering with their effectiveness. This self-assessment may be formal or informal. Informal assessments may take the form of a team member simply asking, "How are we doing?" and "How can we improve our team?"

If you have more time, a group discussion at a team meeting can be a quick and effective exercise for a team.

Some good questions for such an exercise are

- What are our strengths?
- What are we doing well?
- What things should we stop doing because they are reducing our effectiveness?
- What should we begin doing that would increase our effectiveness?
- What things should we continue doing because they are helpful?

If you have more time, you can add additional questions that focus on specific areas of team functioning:

- How can we improve our team meetings?
- What changes do we need to make to our list of ground rules?
- How do you feel about the level of trust and open communication?
- How would you assess our decision-making process?
- To what extent are roles of team members clear and understood by all members of the team?
- How would you describe our relationships with key stakeholders?
- How effective is our ability to resolve differences among members of the team?
- How would you describe the "climate" on this team?

If the team is also cross-functional, cross-cultural, and virtual, you may want to add some questions that address these issues:

- How effective are we at using teleconferencing and [if applicable] video and web conferencing for our meetings?
- To what extent are members empowered by their functional management to make decisions and commit resources?

- To what extent do functional department managers support the work of the team?
- How would you characterize the cross-cultural communication between team members from various countries?

An assessment can have more structure and depth, as we see in the *Parker Team-Development Survey* (see Resource A). This form uses our twelve team characteristics as the criteria against which the team is evaluated. Team players have a variety of applications at their disposal:

1. Each team member completes the form. A team member or a human resources consultant collects the forms and prepares a summary for presentation and discussion at a team meeting.
2. The form is completed at the end of a team meeting. A group discussion on each of the items follows.
3. An outside facilitator interviews each team member, using the form as a basis for the discussion. The facilitator summarizes the results, presents the findings at a team meeting, and leads a discussion on increasing team effectiveness.

The Ineffective Team

Poorly functioning teams are not just the mirror image of effective teams. A team may rank high on some of the dimensions but may not be addressing several critical areas. The stage of development also determines the critical needs of the team, and if those needs are not met the team will not be successful.

For example, in the early stages, a team needs direction and agreement on mission and goals. Therefore, although there may be an informal climate, open communication, and good listening among members, the team will still be considered ineffective if it lacks clear goals and a project plan. In a later stage when conflicts arise, a set of goals buttressed by hard-working, task-oriented members may not be sufficient. The team may fail because they lack good process skills to successfully resolve differences among the members. (See Chapter Six for a description of the stages of team development and what team players can do to adapt successfully to each stage.) A number of warning signs indicate the potential for team difficulties.

Trouble Ahead: The Warning Signs

We conclude this chapter with some factors that may signal problems for your team along with suggestions for addressing the issues.

You Cannot Easily Describe the Team's Purpose or Goals. The development of a clear purpose or mission, including team goals, is especially important in the early stages of a team's history. However, the lack of a clear purpose and performance objectives may also be a problem when the team has been together for many years and they have lost their focus. One other test: if you can articulate the team's purpose, would other team members agree with you? And finally: if the purpose or mission is clear, has the team taken the next important step, which is to create a series of specific performance objectives?

The Meetings Are Formal or Tense. People do not do their best work in an uncomfortable atmosphere. Although people may be somewhat reserved during the first few meetings as they assess the situation, be wary if things do not relax after a reasonable period of time. And you might ask yourself whether anyone on the team is making an effort to develop an informal climate.

There Is a Great Deal of Participation but Little Accomplishment. Some teams exhibit a lot of talk but not much action. They seem to enjoy the interaction that the group provides, but things stall when it is time to take action. If you are a member of a team that has a high level of involvement, ask yourself: are you satisfied with the amount of tangible output or progress toward goals in the last month?

There Is Talk but Not Much Communication. Many teams are composed of very talented people who enjoy talking but do not listen to the contributions of others. Listening is the key to effective planning, problem solving, conflict resolution, and decision making. Think about your last team meeting. Did you notice team members asking questions for clarification, paraphrasing to ensure understanding, or summarizing other members' ideas? If yours is a global, multicultural team and the meetings are conducted in English, do you notice that certain members are not engaged in the discussions?

Disagreements Are Aired in Private Conversations After the Meeting. Although occasionally there are flare-ups in public, rarely are organizational differences brought out into the open. Healthy teams have open discussions of professional differences. Reflect for a moment. Are you aware of important differences among team members that are expressed in informal conversations outside of the meeting but not openly addressed in an appropriate forum?

Decisions Tend to Be Made by the Formal Leader, with Little Meaningful Involvement of Other Team Members. Since many modern leaders are aware of the emphasis on participation, there is a greater use today of brainstorming, surveys, and other methods to obtain team-member involvement. However, the real test is whether everyone's ideas are solicited and seriously considered in an effort to reach a true consensus.

Members Are Not Open with Each Other Because Trust Is Low. In the early stages, a low level of trust is expected as members get to know each other. Trust and open communication are especially critical factors in cross-cultural virtual teams. Therefore, if your team has been together for some time, it would be appropriate to ask whether you (and other members) feel comfortable airing your true feelings about issues that come up.

There Is Confusion or Disagreement About Roles or Work Assignments. Conflicts often surface as interpersonal, emotional issues. In other words, people are just plain mad because another team member has done something or failed to do something. Role conflicts are difficult to see. It may require you to sit down with the other team members and discuss whether the expectations of the roles of all team members are clear and unambiguous.

People in Other Parts of the Organization Who Are Critical to the Success of the Team Are Not Cooperating. Teams usually require the assistance of external people who provide funds, equipment, staff, information, and access. There is rarely a period in a team's history when good external relations are not important. At any point, it is crucial to ask whether there are important stakeholders out there who do not know what we are doing or who are aware of our work but are not supportive.

The Team Is Overloaded with People Who Have the Same Team Player Style. Although there may be diversity in technical expertise, functional knowledge, and culture, there is often a similarity in approaches to teamwork. Style diversity leads to looking at all aspects of team effectiveness. If you suspect a lack of style diversity on your team, consider whether members are equally concerned about completing tasks in a highly professional manner, setting goals and ensuring all work is directed toward those goals, developing and maintaining the group as a team, and candidly questioning goals and methods.

The Team Has Been in Existence for at Least Three Months and Has Never Assessed Its Team Process. It is not uncommon for a team to evaluate progress toward its goals. However, rarely, if ever, does a team take the time to assess its internal team process. Look around at your team and ask, "When was the last time we took a hard look at ourselves?"

Building Your Team

The first step in the process of increasing the effectiveness of your team is to assess the current state of the team. The twelve dimensions of team effectiveness provide the framework, and the *Parker Team-Development Survey*, found in Resource A, provides the vehicle.

Prior to the administration of the survey, the team should review each of the twelve characteristics to arrive at an understanding of the meaning of each item in the context of your team. Bring the framework to life by asking questions such as these:

- How would effective listening skills help us?
- What would open communication look like on our team?
- What are clear roles that are important for our team?
- How would effective relationships with our stakeholders help us?

When the survey is distributed, team members should be asked to provide examples to explain their ratings. These examples will add meaning to the discussion and provide the basis for an improvement plan.

Team members should be asked to share these responses and to discuss the reasons for their answers. Here is where the examples will be helpful. You will find that the discussion of the results will reflect many of the issues included in the survey (listening, open communication, civilized disagreement, consensus decisions). For example, when analyzing the survey results, at some point during the discussion you may want to ask, "Are we using good listening skills?"

Finally, this exercise should lead to an identification of your strengths as a team. It is important to highlight these areas and then to look for ways to support them in the future. Weaknesses also should be identified, followed by analysis and development of an action plan to improve each area.

Team development requires taking a hard look at the current effectiveness of your organization. Our twelve characteristics provide a framework to direct the effort.

The effective team is equally concerned with getting the job done and how the job gets done—both the means and the end. A team needs to think strategically about the future and about its role in the organization. At the same time, the effective team is building and maintaining a positive internal climate.

Effective teams require effective team players. Each of the dimensions of the effective team is furthered by the actions of effective team players. In the next chapter, the characteristics of the effective team player are described and linked to the success of the team.

Notes

1. For more ideas on facilitating teleconferences and video conferences, see Parker and Hoffman, 2006.

2. Sources for such items include www.trainerswarehouse.com and www.creativelearningtools.com.

3. For a review of all team decision-making approaches, see "How to Make a Decision" in Parker and Hoffman (2006).

3

EFFECTIVE TEAM PLAYERS

A team player isn't an isolated example. It's a way
of life that is exhibited in everything they do—
including others in decisions, sharing, pitching in,
networking, looking for new ways of doing
things, etc.

—*Insurance executive, survey response*

Being a team player is *a way of life.* There are many ways that
people in organizations can contribute to the success of a team,
but in the past we have had a limited, often one-dimensional view
of the team player.

In sports, the team player throws the great block that allows
the halfback to score the winning touchdown, makes the beautiful
pass that leads to the important basket, or plays while injured in
the championship game.

In business, the team player supports the company program
without making waves, does the behind-the-scenes work necessary
for the big presentation, or drives through a snowstorm to make a
delivery to a customer.

We now know that teamwork and being a team player are
more complex. The project teams at Chrysler who are designing
and manufacturing new models, the drug development teams at
Merck who are bringing new compounds to market, the research
and development teams at Calgon and Coors who are reducing the
time it takes to commercialize a new product all require a rich combination of the dimensions of effective teamwork. Although all of

the elements are not present in every case, a few characteristics stand out:

- Clear goals and a plan to achieve them
- Positive relationships with and support from other parts of the organization
- Excellent communication, openness, and trust among team members
- A blend of people, each contributing a special talent

Teamwork requires team players. It sounds like a cliché, but it is a central theme of this work that effective teamwork is based on an effective mix of people who exhibit a variety of styles or approaches to teamwork. In our description of the characteristics of an effective team, we called this *style diversity*. In this chapter, we will explore the various styles in some detail.

The Concept of Personal Style

Anyone who thinks about the concept of styles owes an intellectual debt to the psychological theorist Carl Jung. Jung wanted to demystify psychology and create a practical approach to the description of individuals. Jung (1923) called them *psychological types*. Jung's types result from a combination of two attitudes—introversion and extroversion—and four functions—(1) thinking, (2) feeling, (3) sensation, and (4) intuition.

Jung combined the attitudes and functions and created eight psychological types. Although it is not important to describe Jung's types in detail, it is significant to note how he saw the types manifesting themselves in the real world. Jung's principles provide a useful backdrop for the application of our team player styles:

1. The types are categories in which people with similar but not necessarily the same characteristics are found.

2. A person may exhibit one type in one situation and another type in another situation, but he or she usually has one type that predominates in most situations.

3. Each person has the capacity to exhibit all types. In other words, none of the attitudes and functions is missing from anyone.

4. A person's unique combination of characteristics that identify him or her as a particular type is subject to change. Jung believed that the pressures to change were external (parents, society), but we have come to believe changes can be self-directed.

The Myers-Briggs Type Indicator (MBTI) is an instrument used to classify people according to Jungian types (Briggs and Myers, 1957). The MBTI has been extensively validated and is widely used. Although the MBTI was developed primarily as an aid in counseling, it has also been used by many for management and team development. Many other style instruments have been developed for use in organizational settings. They focus on styles of decision making, leadership, and interpersonal relationships (Rowe and Mason, 1987; Atkins, 1981). But there are no research-based instruments that focus on team player styles.

Team Player Styles

Our research indicates four types or styles of team players (see Figure 3.1). Each style contributes in different ways to the success of the team, and each style has a downside when carried to an extreme, as we shall see in the next chapter.

Each of us has the capacity to be an effective team player but in different ways. You and I both can be positive team players and yet act in very different fashions. For example, you may be willing to learn a new system and take on an added responsibility that is needed by the team. I may help by encouraging some of the quiet people to get involved in the discussions or by using

Figure 3.1 Four Team Player Styles

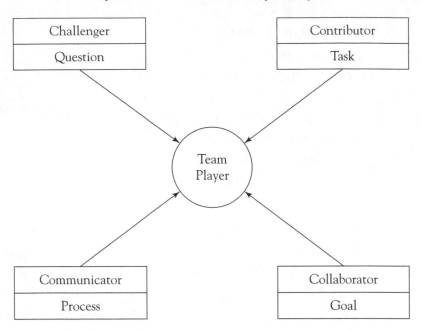

humor to reduce conflicts in the group. Another team member may recommend that we develop goals and an action plan, and someone else may insist that we take a critical look at one of our favorite projects.

We begin the discussion of the four team player styles by presenting a brief summary of each one. The brief style summaries are followed by detailed descriptions. As you review the characteristics that describe each style, think about your primary team at work.

- Which of these descriptions best identifies your primary style?
- Which descriptions best fit your colleagues?

A *Contributor* is a task-oriented team member who enjoys providing the team with good technical information and data, does his or her homework, and then pushes the team to set high performance standards and to use their resources wisely. Most people see the Contributor as dependable.

A *Collaborator* is a goal-directed member who sees the vision, mission, or goal of the team as paramount but is flexible and open to new ideas, is willing to pitch in and work outside his or her defined role, and is able to share the limelight with other team members. Most people see the Collaborator as a strategic, "big picture" person.

A *Communicator* is a process-oriented member who is an effective listener and facilitator of involvement, conflict resolution, consensus building, feedback, and the building of an informal, relaxed climate. Most people see the Communicator as a positive people person.

A *Challenger* is a member who questions the goals, methods, and even the ethics of the team, is willing to disagree with the leader and others, and encourages the team to take well-conceived risks. Most people appreciate the value of the Challenger's candor and openness.

Contributor

A task-oriented team member, the Contributor sees his or her role as providing the group with the best possible information. In the Contributor's view, effective team problem solving and decision making result from the sharing of team members' expertise. The Contributor sees a team as a group of subject matter experts who are expected to complete a series of task assignments. The success of the team is determined by (1) a strong leader who ensures that tasks are distributed among team members and (2) members who finish their assignments in a timely and complete fashion.

Contributors help their teams by freely offering all the relevant knowledge, skills, and data they possess. They realize they are members of the team because they have certain information about the business or about a functional area—information they are expected to contribute. The complex nature of many businesses today requires the use of cross-functional teams to solve problems and meet customer needs. At Digital Equipment Corporation (DEC), cross-functional teams work together to provide customers with integrated solutions; at Merck and Company, multidisciplinary teams come together to develop new drugs. Effective Contributors are critical to the success of these teams. As a human resources professional at DEC put it: "Team players know their own business and that of other key players in other parts of the company who will make things happen."

Freely sharing their expertise means that they do not hold back or hoard information. In some competitive environments, team players withhold technical knowledge from their colleagues because they fear the loss of an "edge" in annual performance appraisals. Some corporate cultures foster this dysfunctional behavior by pitting employees against each other, although some people bring this competitive, anti-teamwork mentality to the workplace themselves. There are specific strategies for addressing this organizational problem, which will be outlined in Chapter Eight.

The sharing of information by the Contributor is expressed in a number of positive ways. A number of our survey respondents pointed to the teaching or training of other team members as an important characteristic of a team player. A Cummins Engine Company's engineer puts "training new team members" in a manufacturing environment at the top of the list. One of our survey respondents reported this vignette of an effective team player at Johnson & Johnson Consumer Products Company:

> A line manager volunteered to serve as an instructor for a quality education workshop. He ordered and assembled the training materials, arrived at class early to help set up and volunteered to stay late to assist. He kept all his commitments, maintained an upbeat attitude throughout, and, after the course, sent his fellow instructors memos telling them what a nice job they did, with copies sent to their bosses.

People's expertise is usually the main reason they are hired and promoted and, generally, is why they are valued in the company.

It is how they are known. It is what sets them apart from other people in the organization. Therefore, to share the very thing that determines your value is to make a significant contribution as a team player. For this reason, the Contributor's role as a trainer or mentor is highly valued.

The "sharing" dimension of the Contributor is seen in the diligence with which all team assignments are completed. The Contributor is someone who sees assignments to collect data, conduct studies, and prepare reports as obligations to be met. Contributors attack these tasks with intensity because they see them as major opportunities to be positive team players. They believe that successful task completion is the key to a success-ful team. In fact, they often become impatient with other team members who do not approach their assignments with the same fervor. In the new team environment, Contributors quickly build a climate of trust because they can be counted on to deliver on their commitments.

There are some downside risks to this aspect of the Contrib-utor. For example, one of our survey respondents from a relocation division of a major corporation sees being a team player as "giving up one's own time and resources to assist others without any direct 'what's in it for me' attitude, *while still completing their own work."* There will be negative implications, he points out in his survey response, if Contributors do not complete their regular respon-sibilities while they are assisting other people. The other people in the work area who must complete the unfinished tasks of the Contributors become resentful. This is especially true if the Con-tributors are being lauded by others as being "outstanding team players" for their helpful actions.

In the new world of cross-functional teams, effective team players contribute to their teams, but they also complete all work in the functional job area. They do not use their team tasks as an excuse to sidestep functional work assignments. This behavior is especially important in companies that make heavy use of cross-functional teams. Balancing the team's need for data to solve problems with the department's need to have its work completed is a tricky but important trait of a successful Contributor.

Effective team players have a clear sense of priorities. They know and are able to rank the myriad of tasks before them. Because, as one manager pointed out, "Team players usually do not say 'no' to requests," they are able to prioritize those requests. In addition, they set realistic deadlines for their deliverables. The Contributor hates to disappoint the other team members and therefore sometimes experiences difficulties serving the needs of two organizations. When conflicts exist, the Contributor looks to the cross-functional team leader to provide direction in regard to the relative importance of the various projects. The Contributor has a low tolerance for ambiguity and will make a priority decision if no direction is provided by the leader.

During the 1940s and 1950s, a New York Yankees baseball player, Tommy Hendrick, was called "Old Reliable" by his teammates. Hendrick seemed to do what was necessary to win the game—make a great catch in a critical situation or hit a home run in the bottom of the ninth inning. He was *dependable*. And that same adjective is often used to describe effective team players. They are the people the team turns to when quality and timeliness are important. The Contributor does not let the team down.

The manner in which information is shared is equally important. The Contributor takes great care to prepare the information he or she presents to the team. No last-minute, slipshod, handwritten, unedited reports from this person. The Contributor's presentations—oral or written—are professionally prepared and delivered. Contributors invest great effort in the project, and they invest equally in the presentation because they want their colleagues to give serious consideration to their work. Effective Contributors also "cleanse" their presentation of arcane jargon, colloquialism, and sports analogies to more clearly communicate with people from different cultures.

Contributors set high personal standards for work and push the team to establish and live up to superior measures. They use words like *quality* and *excellence* and *results* to describe their expectations. Contributors have low tolerance for shortcuts in research, compromises in quality, and incomplete data. They believe their work is thorough and complete, and they insist that other team members hold to the same high standards. Professionalism is highly valued by the Contributor.

Given the emphasis on high standards, it is not surprising that the Contributor believes strongly in "accepting responsibility for one's actions and their consequences," as one engineer said in his response to our survey. What he has in mind is standing up and being held accountable. The team concept sometimes allows people to hide in the shadow of others when problems arise, when deadlines are missed, and when results are questioned. Contributors expect to take responsibility for their work and to answer to their colleagues for the results of their efforts. And they expect the same standard to be applied to all members of the team. In fact, Contributors are likely to initiate accountability discussions when their work is under consideration.

Contributors also value efficiency. Team efficiency means judicious use of time and resources. Everyone is concerned about wasting time, but the Contributor will insist that the team make a special effort to minimize the amount of time spent in meetings; to use alternatives such as email, web conferencing, and online editing tools; and to optimize the time actually spent in those meetings. They push the team to establish a well-thought-out agenda (including time allocations), to limit the length of presentations, to encourage the use of subgroups, and to recommend efficient alternatives to a formal meeting. In the era of teleconferencing and video conferencing, the Contributor will arrive at or call-in to the meeting early or offer to take responsibility for the team to ensure the technology is working well.

Contributor: A Summary

Contributors provide the team with the valuable technical expertise it needs to solve problems and meet its goals. They provide the data, and they provide it in a manner in which it can be easily used. And they often serve as trainers and mentors of other team members. They help the team set high standards, define priorities, and make efficient use of team meeting time and resources.

Contributor: A Checklist of Behaviors

1. Freely shares all relevant information and opinions with other team members
2. Helps the team use its time and resources
3. Pushes the team to set high standards and to achieve top-level results and insists on high-quality outputs
4. Completes all team assignments and other relevant homework necessary for the completion of team tasks
5. Accepts responsibility for all actions as a team member
6. Completes all work in his or her regular job area and all other tasks not related to the team
7. Provides the team with clear, concise, and useful presentations at team meetings
8. Provides technical training for other team members and serves as a mentor for new team members
9. Has a clear set of priorities
10. Develops skills and expertise in the use of web-based tools, teleconferencing, and video conferencing

Contributor: A Checklist of Adjectives

1. Dependable
2. Responsible
3. Organized
4. Efficient
5. Logical
6. Clear

7. Relevant

8. Pragmatic

9. Systematic

10. Proficient

Collaborator

A goal-directed player, the Collaborator sees the vision, goal, or current task as paramount in all interactions. The Collaborator is constantly reminding the team to stay on track and to make sure everything is focused on the target—bringing the drug to market, completing the new system on time, or meeting the production schedule.

Collaborators are willing to work outside their defined roles to get the work done. They never say, "That's not my job," or "My boss won't approve it." In his response to our survey, one Johnson & Johnson employee told us he sees team players as having the "ability and willingness to do work that will benefit the team effort that is outside their area of expertise." He cites the example of a new product team that worked all night loading trucks with product to meet a test-market deadline.

"Pitching in" is a phrase many people use to describe the collaborative team player. Examples abound:

- The bank branch manager who opens another teller's window when a long line of customers are waiting
- The vice president of personnel who is collating manuals the night before the launch of a new training program
- The analyst who canceled a vacation because she got a telephone call about a system problem the night before her scheduled departure

A human resources manager at a bank in Connecticut says it very directly in her response to our survey: "Team players pitch in and help others when they need assistance." In his survey response,

Peter Block, organization development consultant and author of *The Empowered Manager* (1987), simply says, "They cover for each other."

Linked with a willingness to pitch in is the willingness to share the limelight, a characteristic repeatedly cited by our survey respondents. A CEO of a bank reported on "a major investment with great results which was conceived by one executive but he shared the congratulations and results with a committee of team players who got equal credit."

Sharing the limelight may mean working behind the scenes— in effect, not getting any "light" at all. Team players may collect the data, write the reports, draft the speeches, prepare the visuals for a presentation, take responsibility for team meeting logistics, make a special effort to learn a new language, or handle a myriad of other things required for accomplishment of a team's task. Collaborative people regularly perform in this fashion.

"Team players can set aside their own egos when necessary" is the way a telecommunications industry manager put it. Team players derive satisfaction from being part of a successful team rather than just being good individual contributors. They realize their contributions are necessary for the team's success, but they do not require individual recognition to be satisfied with the work.

All of this behavior suggests a commitment to team goals. When asked to rank a list of team player characteristics, our survey respondents put "commitment to team goals" at the top of the list. In the course of many training workshops, we have asked participants to rank a similar list, and each time the "commitment" characteristic is selected as number one. Another survey respondent captured the essence of this point well when he said, "Team players focus on what's good for the business, not just what's good for them or their department."

This commitment requires a necessary first step and therefore we need to back up before we go forward. Too many teams do not take the time to work through the goal-setting process. Collaborative team players, however, insist that their team establish a clear mission, charter, or project plan before proceeding with the work. A mission or purpose statement specifies your products or services and your customers. In other words, it answers the questions "What do you do?" and "For whom do you do it?" And it is important to understand that a mission is not something just for the top of the house. Every division, department, committee, task force, or other business team should have a clear mission, a reason for being.

Collaborators then help the team develop a set of long-range goals and short-term performance objectives. They want to be part of an organization that is going somewhere—an organization that has a sense of direction and a plan to get there. When required, they may be visionary as well. That is, they encourage the team to take a strategic view—to think about the future, to create what Warren Bennis (1989, p. 20) refers to as a "sense of outcome, goal, or direction" for the organization. Collaborators are uncomfortable with teams that see goal setting as the development of a "to-do" list for the next year. Collaborators will also insist that the team look at the impact of the global marketplace on the team's goals and objectives. They understand that a new product, for example, must be developed with customers in Beijing as well as Boston in mind.

The Collaborator also brings the goal-setting process to the daily environment. Although the big picture is important, the current task is also significant. This team player helps the team understand and clarify its immediate work assignment and even the specific reason for today's meeting. Questions such as "What's our purpose for meeting today?" and "What do we hope to accomplish?" and then, "What is the agenda?" help the team move forward in a systematic fashion (Parker and Hoffman, 2006). At a recent team meeting, the chairperson of a task force seemed poorly prepared for the session. Another member, playing the Collaborator role, got the meeting moving by pulling out the milestone chart and identifying the task assignments that were due that day.

Once vision, mission, goals, objectives, and plans are in place, effective teams take the time to revisit them on a regular basis. Plans may be reviewed daily, weekly, or monthly; objectives should be reviewed monthly or quarterly; and at an annual meeting, teams should assess progress toward goals. The ongoing validity of the mission and vision also may be examined on an annual basis. Collaborators remind the team and even insist that these reviews take place. They know that without periodic reviews, the goal-setting process loses credibility and, even more critical, the inherent value of goal setting is lost to the team.

Committed team players will work toward goals or will complete specific tasks even though they may not agree with them. It is easy to push ahead toward team goals that are aligned with your personal goals or values. However, a litmus test for a real team player is the willingness to work in earnest for a goal that was approved over his or her objections. At a major computer company, six vice presidents worked together to build a three-year strategy for the manufacturing division. As the director of human resources noted in his survey response, "They all knew going in that the outcome would result in some of them losing a piece of their turf and yet they proceeded to work toward implementation."

Closely related to the capability to support all team goals is the need to support the team in all interactions outside the team. Positive team players will argue their points with intensity during the meeting but, win or lose, they will support the outcome. The negative team players will criticize the work of the team and often reveal the details of discussions, intending to embarrass other team members. In the end, the whole team loses because the image of the team is tarnished. As one survey respondent put it, "On effective teams there is a lack of gossip and sabotage." Collaborative team players speak with pride and enthusiasm about their team.

Some teams have adopted the sports analogy of the *practice* field and the *playing* field. The practice field is the team meeting where members discuss, argue, disagree, but ultimately come up with a "game plan" (project plan, decision, or recommendation). The ground rules of the practice field include respect for different points of view, open communication, trust, and, most important, confidentiality. The playing field is where the team *as a united front* presents its plan to the appropriate stakeholders (such as clients, senior management, government regulators).

Collaborators also see the big picture and help the team see how their goals fit with some larger context. As Warren Bennis (1988) reminds us, "Text without context is pretext." The environment, the organization, the global marketplace, and the various cultures in which a team functions have fundamental impacts on success. Collaborators play the role of the team player who regularly reminds the team of where they fit and of the importance of positive interactions with significant players around the world. For most teams, there is a need to manage effectively the interface with other units within the same organization, with people in partner organizations (joint ventures, vendors), with customers, and often with regulatory agencies in a variety of countries.

The Collaborator is open to new ideas and data even when that information may suggest an alteration of team goals and plans. In our survey, "openness to new ideas" was one of the three most frequently mentioned characteristics of an effective team player. In his response to our survey, a vice president of human resources for a chain of newspaper and television stations said he sees a team player as someone who "recognizes the importance of having ideas contributed from various sources and is willing to have an 'open window' and permit those ideas to impact their behavior." In addition, he finds team players to be less rigid and, as a result, more creative and innovative.

When asked for a specific example of a team player, another survey respondent pointed to a vice president who surveyed department employees, requesting input on ways to increase effectiveness in the areas of communications, goals, and other organizational issues. He scheduled meetings to discuss the survey results and, most important, followed up on all suggestions and changes.

At the personal level, the effective Collaborator is open to hearing and doing something about critical feedback. The openness extends to his or her own behavior as a team member. This open posture is typically the outgrowth of a high level of self-esteem. Many people in our survey saw effective team players as secure, confident people who usually feel good about themselves. This characteristic seems to be a necessary condition for openness and for a willingness to change—both organizationally and interpersonally.

Collaborator: A Summary

Collaborators play a key role in keeping a team goal-directed and focused on the steps necessary to reach that goal. They serve as models by working outside their prescribed jobs and being willing to spread around the rewards of team success. In a crisis, they will drop everything to help out other team members. They are open to new ideas that may impact the team's efforts and to feedback about their own performance.

Collaborator: A Checklist of Behaviors

1. Helps the team establish long-term goals and clarify its current objective or task

2. Helps the team see how its work fits into the total organization

3. Regularly reminds the team of the need to revisit their goals and action plans

4. Encourages the team to establish plans with milestones and appropriate task assignments

5. Pitches in to help out other team members who need assistance

6. Works hard to achieve team goals and to complete the current tasks even though he or she may not agree with them

7. Does not gossip about other team members or share negative comments about team process with nonmembers

8. Is flexible and open to new ideas or data that may alter team goals

9. Often works outside his or her defined role to help the team achieve its goals

10. Is willing to share the limelight with other team members

Collaborator: A Checklist of Adjectives

1. Cooperative
2. Flexible
3. Confident
4. Forward-looking
5. Conceptual
6. Accommodating
7. Generous
8. Open
9. Visionary
10. Imaginative

Communicator

The Communicator gives primary emphasis to team process—how the team goes about completing its tasks and reaching its goals. The Communicator believes there is an interpersonal "glue" that must be present for a team to be effective. Although the Communicator's efforts are sometimes resisted by other members (as "touchy-feely stuff"), everyone agrees that teams succeed or fail based on attention to process issues. Despite the fact that our description of the effective team includes many process dimensions (listening, communication, conflict, trust), most people would rather not address these subjects. Team goals, roles, and task assignments are easier issues to confront.

We all know that the climate and culture of a team are critical to the success of the total effort. Climate influences such factors as productivity, creativity, and problem solving. The Communicator contributes to a positive climate by helping people on the team get to know and feel comfortable with each other. This does not mean that everyone's deepest and darkest secrets must be revealed. As a participant recently said to me, "I'm a very private person, and I don't like telling other people about my personal life." I indicated that his statement was sufficiently revealing, and we went on to discuss his work life. Given the new reality of teamwork in today's world, culture is now a very important factor in team success. The ability of a team to understand and use cultural diversity among team members often falls to the Communicator on the team. The Communicator is likely to be the one who recognizes that some members are not participating because other members are speaking too fast, using unfamiliar words, or not including them in the discussions. Communicators will see it as their role to facilitate their participation directly or to make the meeting leader aware of the situation and encourage him or her to address the issue.

The Communicator is especially helpful at the time of team formation—the awkward period when people are waiting for direction. The Communicator is helpful when the composition of the team changes or when a new member joins the team. People simply want to know who the other players are and what they bring to the party. This orientation extends beyond the personal dimension to the skills, resources, and experience each person will contribute to the work of the team. For example, at the first meeting of a major software task force, all members described their past projects, the programming languages they knew, and the systems with which they had experience. This information was posted on flip charts around the room, and the net result was the creation of a team talent bank. In the forming stage, the Communicator facilitates the development of norms or ground rules that define the standards of behavior that are acceptable to all members of the team.

The informal climate that was mentioned as a hallmark of the effective team is facilitated by the Communicator. He or she initiates and supports pre- and post-meeting discussions of nonwork subjects (family, vacations, hobbies, sports) that help create a relaxed atmosphere. Good-natured kidding and comments that break the tension or smooth over an awkward moment contribute to the effectiveness of the team. The opening moments of a teleconference or video conference, when members are entering the room or joining the conversation, are good times for the Communicator to engage everyone in such an informal exchange of trivial information. The Communicator uses humor, tact, and even diplomacy to encourage informality and to reduce destructive conflict. As Cathie Black of *USA Today* put it, "Humor is a great gift because it is a great weapon. It deflects hostility, tension and anger" (Cohen, 1989, p. 83).

Another key element of a team's success is the ability of team members to listen to each other. As highlighted in the previous chapter, high-level listening skill is a hallmark of the effective team. The Communicator models this characteristic in many ways. At a recent team meeting, a vice president demonstrated this ability by asking questions to obtain more information or clarification, paraphrasing many of the responses, and taking notes on the answers. He sent a simple, direct, and powerful message about the importance of listening to the other players on his team. Active listening was especially important in this case, because many team members were based in European cities and English was not their primary language. However, later they reported that the behavior of the vice president encouraged them to participate because he seemed to be very interested in what they had to say.

Effective Communicators listen to the complete story. They refrain from interrupting presentations or comments by other team members, and often they will caution others to do the same. They work hard to withhold judgment until all the facts and opinions are outlined and the conclusions presented. Good listeners are valued as team members because of what they contribute to positive team process. They are also valued because listening is a skill that is in short supply.

Communicators are not laid-back, *laissez-faire* participants. They believe, as one of our survey respondents said, "Communication is not a spectator sport." Good Communicators are active. They step in and take an active role when ineffectual process is standing in the way of goal attainment. Communicators encourage quiet members to give their opinions, ask the more talkative people to give other members an opportunity to share their views, request that members confine their disagreements to the subject and eliminate personal attacks, and suggest that the team establish certain norms or guidelines for team interactions. They are especially sensitive to the importance of cultural differences in team communications and the resulting necessity that the communication norms on the team be adapted to the fact that English is not the primary language of many team members. For example, the Communicator may suggest that all communication be specific and clear, with minimal jargon, colloquialisms, and sports analogies.

These interventions can be risky; but as with all risks, the payoffs can be great. Another series of risky interventions concerns feedback—both the giving and the receiving of comments about behavior as a team player. Effective team players tend to be confident people with a high level of self-esteem. Therefore they are able to receive feedback about their performance without becoming defensive. As another Johnson & Johnson manager observed in his survey response, "Team players show a willingness to hear and do something about critical feedback." In fact, they will often initiate a conversation in which they solicit feedback about their performance.

Communicators also offer feedback to other team members about their participation on the team. Effective team players know how to offer comments that are specific, intended to be helpful, and expressed in a manner such that the other person will be able to hear and use it. Feedback is a process that requires skill and courage.

Communicative team players are active in other ways. They project enthusiasm about the team's work, about progress toward the goal, and about accomplishments along the way. They are positive people. For them, the glass is half full rather than half empty. Failures are opportunities to learn. They have, as one survey respondent from AT&T put it, "a can-do attitude." She went on to say that team players are "energy givers rather than energy users." Communicators have the ability to persevere and to spread that energy to other team players. When teams are performing well, the competitive cohesion that develops is usually fostered by the Communicator. Team members feel good about their team, and a friendly competition develops with other teams.

This enthusiasm extends to a sense of urgency about the work of the team. Communicators spur the team to move forward with their work. They are able to establish and maintain the necessary momentum to sustain a team over a long period. This sense of movement is extremely important, because teams usually experience an ebb and flow that includes periods of great progress mixed with times of slow growth and setbacks. Layoffs, reorganizations, budget cuts, negative results, and changing priorities all affect team climate. Teams need key players who will urge them to move ahead during these periods.

Team members need recognition and praise for their efforts, and Communicators have a knack for when to deliver this message. They know that recognition usually costs nothing and therefore they are not stingy with it. In a recent survey I conducted for a company, "lack of recognition for performance" was cited as the major employee complaint. People said they wanted some form of recognition beyond a salary increase, including such things as positive verbal feedback or a commendation letter sent to their manager. Communicators are usually ready with a "good job" or a "thanks for the extra effort" at a meeting or with an email message about a presentation or report.

The ongoing praise should be supplemented by larger recognition events when milestones are reached or when significant outcomes are achieved. The Communicator will urge the team to take the time to celebrate their accomplishments and recognize members. The new world of teams requires that teams find creative ways of recognizing member contributions. The Communicator is the person who helps make this happen.

We propose the consensus method as the preferred approach to decision making in certain critical team situations. However, a consensus does not just suddenly emerge because we want it to happen; this is when the Communicator plays a critical role. He or she will encourage participation from everyone, discourage voting, bring out the reasons behind opinions, ask for data or prior experience with the issue, and summarize the key points. The summary may form the basis for a consensus, or it may simply point out the areas of agreement and disagreement. At a certain time, the Communicator will see the basis for consensus and test the waters for possible agreement by saying, for example, "It sounds like most of us agree that customer service is the number-one priority and we should develop a plan for establishing a new customer service department."

Finally, effective team players will recognize the importance of a periodic team self-assessment. They will propose that the team take some time to ask and answer the question "How are we doing?" This review can include a look at progress toward the goals, a check on the milestones, and an evaluation of team process—communication, participation, conflict resolution, and listening. The assessment should conclude with an acknowledgment of successes and a plan for improvement.

Communicator: A Summary

A process-oriented member, the Communicator is an effective listener and facilitator of participation, conflict resolution, consensus building, feedback, and the building of an informal, relaxed climate.

Communicator: A Checklist of Behaviors

1. Steps in to resolve process problems such as conflict among team members or lack of involvement by some members
2. Listens attentively to all viewpoints, while withholding judgment

3. Helps the team relax and have fun by joking, laughing, and discussing personal interests

4. Recognizes and praises other team members for their efforts and helps the leader come up with new ways of acknowledging the contributions of members

5. Communicates enthusiasm and a sense of urgency about the team's work

6. Periodically summarizes the status of a discussion or proposes a possible consensus

7. Encourages other team members to participate in the discussions and decisions of the team, with special attention given to members for whom English is not their primary language

8. Helps the people on the team get to know each other and to know what skills and resources each can contribute

9. Gives feedback to other team members—feedback that is descriptive, specific, and intended to be helpful

10. Receives feedback from other team members without becoming defensive

11. Reminds the team to take the time periodically to assess team effectiveness and plan for improvement

Communicator: A Checklist of Adjectives

1. Supportive

2. Encouraging

3. Relaxed

4. Tactful

5. Helpful

6. Friendly

7. Patient

8. Informal

9. Considerate

10. Spontaneous

Challenger

A colleague told me the following story about a management board meeting of a bank: "At one point during the meeting, the president asked, 'How's morale around here?' The first person to respond was the vice president sitting to the left of the president. He said that on a scale of 10 he would rate morale an 8. The remainder of the vice presidents responded with a 7 or 8. When my turn came, I wanted to tell the truth and say 3 or 4 but I didn't have the courage."

This story illustrates groupthink at its worst. It may be that the vice presidents believed the president did not want to hear bad news and therefore they were simply being good soldiers. In other words, the climate did not support honesty, especially when it required the delivery of unpleasant information. Nevertheless, effective teamwork requires people who will speak out with an honest and authentic voice. This is the role of the Challenger.

Challengers, as one person in our survey reported, are willing to "swim against the tide." They are candid, open, honest, and above all deeply concerned about the direction of the team. And they very much want the team to succeed. However, Challengers may appear to be a negative force on the team, as they express opposition to the prevailing thinking and even to the team leader. But the effective Challenger opposes team direction with good intentions, not merely to be against something.

One key test for the Challenger is the ability to speak out, as in the bank example just cited, even when his or her views are contrary to those of the vast majority of the team. Speaking out is an indication of a team player's strength because the culture of most organizations discourages the expression of minority views. In fact, anti-establishment thoughts are considered the very antithesis of team player behavior. As a result of interviews with one hundred managers in two companies, Robert Jackall (1983, p. 123) found that, "While being a team player has many meanings, one of the most important is to be interchangeable with other managers near one's level. Corporations discourage narrow specialization more strongly as one goes higher. They also *discourage the expression of moral or political qualms.* . . . The public statement of such objection would end any realistic aspirations for higher posts because one's usefulness to the organization depends on versatility" (emphasis added).

Ironically, many Challengers are accused of not being team players because they raise objections to team decisions. If the corporate norm about teamwork is "To get along, go along," then the Challenger will not be accepted as a team player. However, in that kind of culture, being accused of not being a team player is a sure sign of a courageous Challenger.

Disagreeing with the team leader is one of the most difficult acts for the Challenger. It is difficult because the leader is by definition in a position of authority and often is higher in the official corporate hierarchy as well. As one person said to me when I suggested that he say something to the chairperson about a problem, "Are you crazy? She's got too many Hay points!" (translation: she holds a higher position). However, at a meeting at another company a few weeks later, I saw a team member challenge a position taken by the chairperson. The chairperson reacted well to the comment, suggesting that it was a view he had not considered. The impact on the other team members was dramatic. It freed them to increase both the quality and the depth of their participation. Honesty is potent.

The Challenger will also raise questions about the team's fundamental mission and goals. At management meetings at a major computer company, I have heard team members voice their strong opposition to the corporate goal of becoming a key player in a new global market. This was a brave act because the decision to proceed had been made at the top of the house. As one survey respondent pointed out to me, "A team player must be willing to speak out when the corporation may be making a decision which may appear to be correct but in principle is inconsistent with our long-term goals."

At team meetings, the effective team player will not be reluctant to ask pointed questions about reports and presentations. A Challenger wants to know

- Why certain things are being done
- Whether alternatives have been considered
- The costs versus the benefits
- The impacts on customers
- How employees will be affected
- Whether something can be tried out on a pilot basis
- Whether the environmental impact has been considered
- Whether it will work in certain global markets
- Whether we have trained staff to provide the after-sale service
- Whether government regulators will approve it

Often the Challenger will make other team members feel uncomfortable. The questions and disagreements may point out lack of preparation, failure to review a problem thoroughly, or questionable integrity. Although almost everyone would agree intellectually with the need for these issues to be raised, in practice many members probably wish the Challenger would just go away. As one person said to me in describing a Challenger in his company, "He's really a pain in the butt." In fact, many Challengers are stereotyped as the iconoclast or "weirdo." But for many people, "honest and authentic" is the best way to describe the Challenger. As team players, they are factual and truthful in reporting results, and they expect other members to be the same. They are also open about problems facing the team—including their own contributions. Challengers push the team to talk openly about quality problems, budget overruns, customer complaints, cultural differences, employee dissatisfaction, and missed deadlines.

Closely aligned with the need for open discussion of team progress and problems is the need for maintaining the confidentiality of the discussions. The Challenger, like the Collaborator, believes that these discussions should not be the subject of gossip and loose talk outside of team meetings. Strict ground rules regarding frank deliberations need to be established so team members will feel free to be open and candid.

The Challenger is a highly ethical person who encourages the team to set high ethical standards for their work. He or she will insist that the team behave as follows:

- Be truthful, sincere and forthright and not lie, cheat, or deceive
- Be honorable, principled and courageous and not adopt an "end justifies the means" philosophy
- Keep promises, fulfill commitments, and not interpret agreements in an overly technical or legalistic manner in order to escape compliance
- Be open-minded, treat people equally, tolerate diversity and not take unfair advantage of another person's difficulties
- Accept responsibility for their decisions and the consequences of their activities ["Ethical Values and Principles," 1988, p. 153]

Again, insistence on high ethical standards does raise the discomfort level of some other team members. This is the role of the Challenger.

Pushed to the extreme, the Challenger becomes a whistle-blower who will go public with illegal and unethical team actions. The effective Challenger will be a good team player and try to resolve the issue in the context of the team or with the leadership of the team. In other words, Challengers will exhaust all internal avenues of negotiation before taking the issue to an outside forum. And they will remain ethical in their pursuit of the issue. They will not bring charges against the team to obtain publicity, to settle a grudge, or in some other way to gain personally from their actions.

In fact, just the reverse is likely to result. They may lose their jobs and be branded as troublemakers.

A famous corporate Challenger comes to mind: Jerome J. LiCari, director of research and development at Beech-Nut Nutrition Corporation. LiCari discovered that the apple juice concentrate sold to Beech-Nut by a supplier contained little or no juice. Beech-Nut was selling the apple juice for babies as "100% fruit juice with no sugar added." Via memos, reports, and meetings with his superiors, LiCari tried for four years to get the company to act on the evidence. At one point, LiCari's supervisor told him that *he was not being a team player* and threatened that if he continued to pursue this issue, he would be fired. Finally, in 1982, some four years after he first discovered the adulterated concentrate, he resigned. Ultimately, two Beech-Nut executives were convicted of selling the bogus product, sentenced to one year in jail, and each fined $100,000. The company was fined $2 million. The company also settled a civil suit in the amount of $7.5 million (Traub, 1988).

Challengers will also push the team to be more creative in their problem solving. Challengers encourage their team to not be bound by the past or other restrictions but to use brainstorming to generate a free flow of new ideas. They will ask the team to set aside the "killer phrases" that stifle creativity:

- "We tried that last year."
- "Our boss won't buy it."
- "It's not in the budget."
- "That's not our job."

Effective team players cringe when they hear these phrases and will challenge the team to override these objections or, better still, not to raise or discuss them until the ideation stage is complete. "Let the good ideas flow" is the theme of the Challengers. They know that a climate that encourages risk taking is necessary for real innovation to take place. Challenging team players have an important role in pushing the team to take well-considered risks. A recent study of group decision making reported that groups with a high rate of dissent produced higher-quality solutions than groups without dissent (Schultz-Hardt and others, 2006).

The real mark of effective Challengers is their knowing when to stop pushing. If you are a real team player, you know when a consensus has emerged and when it is time to move on. Team players will say, "I've had my day in court, all sides of the issues have been discussed, and the team has reached a genuine agreement." A real team player supports the consensus and works toward its implementation unless a real legal or ethical concern remains.

The Challenger who does not know when to quit or when to acknowledge resolution of the issue can be a destructive force on the team. The perennial devil's advocate is not a positive team player.

Challenger: A Summary

The Challenger is a team player who openly questions the goals, methods, and even the ethics of the team; who is willing to disagree with the team leader; and who encourages the team to take well-considered risks.

Challenger: A Checklist of Behaviors

1. Candidly shares views about the work of the team
2. Is willing to disagree openly with the leadership of the team
3. Often raises questions about the team's goals
4. Pushes the team to set high ethical standards for work
5. Speaks out even when views are contrary to those of a vast majority of the team
6. Asks "why?" and "how?" and other relevant questions about presentations at team meetings
7. Sometimes is accused of not being a team player because he or she differs with the conventional wisdom

8. Challenges the team to take well-conceived risks

9. Is honest in reporting team progress and stating problems facing the team

10. Is willing to blow the whistle on illegal and unethical activities of the team

11. Will back off when views are not accepted and will support a legitimate team consensus

Challenger: A Checklist of Adjectives

1. Candid

2. Ethical

3. Questioning

4. Honest

5. Truthful

6. Outspoken

7. Principled

8. Adventurous

9. Aboveboard

10. Brave

Team Player Actions

Teams need many things to be successful, and a variety of team player styles is one important dimension of effective teamwork. Conversely, a team player can contribute in many ways to the success of a team. There is no one clear description of a team player. A team player comes in a variety of uniforms with varied equipment.

The message for team players is this: "Affirm your style, your strengths, your specific contributions to the team effort. And do it well. Be the best Contributor, Collaborator, Communicator, or

Challenger. In addition, recognize that you have the capacity to make greater use of the strengths of other styles. You can change. If you find that your effectiveness would increase by extending your team player style, then plan and work toward the incorporation of additional strengths into your repertoire."

In the end, the complete team player is able to use the strengths of all four styles as required by the situation. The situational determinants include the stage of team development (see Chapter Six) and the current team methods (see Chapter Eight).

The *Parker Team Player Survey,* found in Resource C, will give you a reading on your current primary team player style. As you reflect on your behavior in teams, try to identify some situations that would be aided by actions associated with other styles. For example, my primary style is Communicator. A committee of which I am a member is overloaded with many other process people. The group clearly lacks someone who is willing to question important decisions. At a recent committee meeting, I extended my team player style by objecting to a proposed decision and insisting that the group consider other alternatives. My opposition brought out similar opinions by other committee members who had been reluctant to speak out. Although it was not easy to behave in an unfamiliar fashion, the result was satisfying. Clearly, it will be easier next time. It will also be easier for the other team members who saw the value of another style.

The message for corporate executives and high-level managers is this: "Expand your view of the team player to include all four dimensions—task, goal, process, and questioning. As you make decisions about team composition, team leadership, succession planning, and performance appraisal, consider this broader conception of the team player. And stop thinking of a team player as someone who simply 'fits in' and who will not 'rock the boat'."

In Chapter Eight, we describe methods of creating an organizational culture that supports positive team players.

4

INEFFECTIVE TEAM PLAYERS

Sometimes we try too hard to help the team. We are so committed to the team effort, so absorbed in our view of what the team needs, that we become ineffective. We overemphasize the importance of task completion, goal direction, process, or challenging the status quo. Even though we have the best of intentions, we get to the point that Stuart Atkins called "too much of a good thing" (Atkins, 1981).

The team may be doing well and the team players may seem to be doing well when, almost without notice, one will go over the boundary. The effective team player becomes a drain on the team. The helpful comments are now barriers to success. In this case, there is such a thing as too much help—too much team play.

Some team members are particularly committed to one of our four styles. They believe that they have the key to a successful team. One negative result of this strong commitment is the inability to see clearly the usefulness of the other styles. These players may become impatient with team players who are trying to be helpful in *other* ways. Overly committed team players may exaggerate the dimensions of their own styles and push the team to do the same. Stresses such as time pressure, deadlines, and decreased revenues can lead to a lack of tolerance for other team players. Ironically, these are just the times when we need more effective team play.

The motivations for behavior are many and complex. Our purpose here is not to root out all causes of ineffective team players.

However, observation tells us that some people try too hard to be helpful and, as a result, go beyond the zone of effectiveness. Their strength becomes a weakness. Observation also teaches us that the pressures of business lead to an impatience with alternative team player styles. Style differences are seen as blocks to progress. On the other hand, some people have never learned how to be an effective team player. See Exhibit 4.1 for a list of questions to help you determine whether you are an ineffective team player.

Exhibit 4.1 Are You an Ineffective Team Player?

Read each question and fill in a letter for your response:
Yes (Y), Sometimes (S), No (N)

_____ 1. When forming a new team, do you select only those people whose approaches are similar to yours?

_____ 2. When things are not going your way, do you sit quietly or sulk?

_____ 3. Are you impatient with other team members who want to discuss process issues?

_____ 4. Do you try to avoid or smooth over differences among team members?

_____ 5. Do you go along with some team decisions even though you are not sure going along is the right thing to do?

_____ 6. As a team leader, do you set goals without the real involvement of team members?

_____ 7. When things go wrong on the team, do you quickly blame the leader?

_____ 8. Do you criticize the team to other people in the organization?

_____ 9. Do you miss deadlines for completion of team assignments or submit incomplete work?

_____ 10. Do you push for individual recognition of team members rather than team acknowledgment and awards?

Summary: If you answered "no" to all ten questions, skip to the next chapter.

If you answered "yes" or "sometimes" to at least five questions, stay tuned.

If you answered "yes" to all ten questions, start the book over again.

The Cost of Ineffective Team Players

Ineffective team players cost the organization. Their behavior results in wasted time and effort, lost opportunities, poor customer relations, low morale, and high turnover. Ultimately, they have a negative impact on the bottom line. In mortgage banking, for example, loan originators who are ineffective Communicators fail to build positive relationships with the loan processors. The originators then spend more time on the loan packages and less time originating loans. The net result is decreased sales and usually turnover in the processor support group.

Mergers and acquisitions can be derailed by ineffective team players in key roles during the transition phase. If members of the transition team are not willing to collaborate on goals and plans, to pitch in and do what is necessary for the good of the new organization, and to be concerned about avoiding "throwing the acquisition's existing employees off balance" (Dionne, 1988, p. 16), the outcome can be disastrous in business and human terms.

Software development can be excessively time-consuming, costly, and frustrating without effective team players. Many software developers enjoy working alone and therefore have become ineffective team players. They are Contributors in the extreme. They issue high-quality technical work but sometimes fail to see where the systems fit into the business. And they may have poor interpersonal skills for dealing with users. Often, the outcome is a release that is late, does not meet user requirements, or requires extensive modification.

In the new organizational environment, in which the expectations for teams are much higher than previously, ineffective team players are even more troublesome. Contributors who are perfectionists can paralyze a team, causing them to miss deadlines and incur the anger of senior management. Challengers who refuse to back off an issue even after a consensus has been reached can cause the team to lose credibility with key stakeholders. In addition, because we know that leading teams today—especially cross-functional and cross-cultural teams—is infinitely more difficult than it used to be, ineffective team players simply add another unnecessary barrier to team success.

At a recent committee meeting, a conflict arose over the future direction of the team. The team leader negotiated an agreement with her boss and then announced the decision to the team. The team members disagreed with the decision and were upset about the process used to arrive at the decision. In an effort to smooth over the conflict, a compromise was proposed by one member and quickly supported by the team leader. However, it was a true compromise in the sense that it "split the differences" and satisfied no one. Ineffective team play led to a poor decision. Subsequently, two key people left the team.

The Ineffective Contributor

The task-oriented Contributor who has helped the team by providing useful technical information, by always doing the required homework, and by being a model of excellence can become ineffective because of any of these factors:

- Data overload (reports that are too long and too detailed)
- Pushing for unrealistic performance standards
- Losing sight of the big picture (the goal or charter of the team)
- A lack of patience with the need for a positive team climate
- A failure to appreciate and use cultural differences on a global team

When things go wrong, the Contributor believes the solution is more and better information, reports, and presentations.

Ineffective Contributors abound in technical and scientific organizations. Their battle cry is "Let's be objective." For them, the goal of every business activity is to remove the human element. Therefore, the emphasis is on efficiency, following the rules, being correct, minimizing risk, reducing costs, and increasing the use of technology. As you might suspect, an ineffective Contributor can also be pretty boring.

Contributors often have a very narrow focus on just the work and, specifically, the immediate task or next deliverable. On one long-term product development team, it was suggested that the team should plan a celebration to reward itself for achieving a major milestone about eighteen months into the project and recognize certain members who had made major contributions. Several members argued that "we get paid every other Friday—that's our reward." They failed to see the big picture, the long-term aspects of the project, the motivational value of rewards and recognition, and the importance of maintaining a positive climate on the team.

During a discussion on business ethics, an otherwise effective Contributor went over the line when he persisted in his position that all ethical decisions could be "objectified." He argued that all we needed were "facts" to determine what to do when faced with this dilemma. The problem, as he saw it, was that the situation simply did not provide the team with enough information. Other team members tried to explain that more facts were not going to change their opinions, as they were strongly influenced by personal values and religious beliefs. His insistence on more and better data caused delays and bad feelings among team members.

The Ineffective Contributor: A Checklist of Adjectives

1. Data-bound
2. Shortsighted
3. Narrow
4. Perfectionist
5. Cautious

The Ineffective Collaborator

The goal-directed Collaborator pushes the team to develop a mission and goals and helps by pitching in, sharing resources, working outside his or her defined role, and doing what is required to maintain that commitment to the team goal or charter. But the Collaborator can become ineffective because of any of these factors:

- Failure to revisit and take a hard look at the team mission and goals
- Lack of attention to the immediate team tasks and performance quality
- Failure to focus on the importance of active participation by all members of the team
- Public complaints about team failures

When the team is perceived as decreasingly effective, the Collaborator believes the solution lies in greater commitment to the vision, mission, and goals of the team.

Ineffective Collaborators are typically found in middle management positions in organizations. They have read some books on leadership and think that their role is no longer to manage but to lead. They work hard to be seen as forward-looking and a visionary. In fact, they do a good job of creating a vision, developing a mission statement, and preparing goals. However, the process becomes an end in itself. They fail to realize that the process must be managed. Goals require objectives, action plans, and accountability. As status reports and other follow-up methods are needed to ensure process, the leader shifts to the role of manager. But the ineffective Collaborator has little patience for the work involved in managing the effort.

Ineffective Collaborators are insensitive to other team players who do not give as much attention to goals. They see team players who insist that the team complete the day-to-day work tasks as "grunts." They view Communicators who want to see an effective process for developing goals as "touchy-feely." And they consider Challengers who question the goals to be obstructionists.

Ineffective Collaborators try to do too much. In an effort to be helpful to their colleagues, they jump in and take over from other team members. While the Collaborator sees the action as helpful ("I'm just rolling up my sleeves and pitching in"), other team players see it as unnecessary interference and control.

The Ineffective Collaborator: A Checklist of Adjectives

1. Too future oriented
2. Not task focused
3. Unrealistic
4. Unconcerned about group process
5. A dreamer

The Ineffective Communicator

The process-oriented Communicator who has helped the team by effectively facilitating member involvement, conflict resolution, consensus building, cross-cultural understanding, and other positive climate management activities can become ineffective in ways such as these:

- Seeing team process as an end in itself ("Are we having fun yet?")
- Failing to challenge or confront other team members
- Not recognizing the equal importance of completing task assignments and making progress toward team goals
- Relying too much on humor and other process techniques

When the team fails to make progress, the Communicator assumes the reason must be that "We don't work well together" and proceeds to push for increased emphasis on listening, feedback, and participation.

The ineffective Communicator usually can be found in the human resources department. He or she may have been to some seminars on group dynamics and taken it all in as gospel. For these Communicators, process becomes a new religion. They embrace it with all the fervor of an extremist. They see process problems everywhere, and they see the solution to all the team's ills as better relationships among team members. As a result, they tend to alienate many people who might see the importance of positive process but who realize it is not the only dimension of effective teamwork. The worst thing that can happen to a Communicator who crosses the line and enters the ineffectiveness zone is to not be taken seriously by other team members. Other members wonder about someone who does not appear to be concerned about important team goals and issues. Alternatively, some Communicators refuse to acknowledge conflicts among members, communications break-downs due to cultural and language differences, and tensions arising from lack of trust. They prefer to believe that if there are no overt indications of interpersonal problems, then everything is just fine.

At the first meeting of a new business team, an ineffective Communicator with the best of intentions tried to begin by conducting several exercises designed to develop a positive climate. There was resistance from other team members, but she persisted in carrying out her plan. At the end of the meeting, it was explained to her that the timing was inappropriate. When a new team forms, people want to know something about team purpose, team roles, tentative timetable, management's expectations, and other fundamentals. After they feel comfortable with the task, they will be willing to deal with team process. In this case, the team was so upset it was not possible to discuss team norms and relationships for at least a month.

The Ineffective Communicator: A Checklist of Adjectives

1. Aimless
2. Not sufficiently serious
3. Vague
4. Impractical
5. Not focused on the bottom line

The Ineffective Challenger

The Challenger who helps the team by candidly questioning the team's goals and methods, raising ethical issues, disagreeing with the leadership, and encouraging risk taking can become an ineffective team player in any of these ways:

- Not knowing when to back off and let the team move on
- Pushing the team to take risks that are beyond reason
- Becoming self-righteous, rigid, and inflexible
- Isolating himself or herself to a point where challenging is an end in itself
- Using so-called honesty as a cover for attacks on other team members

When the team is not moving ahead, the Challenger believes that there is a lack of candor or innovativeness and that the solution lies in greater confrontation and risk taking.

The ineffective Challenger is found everywhere, but there seem to be more of them in manufacturing and in the blue-collar areas of government (for example, roads and public safety). We also find them among scientists in basic research. These are people who love a fight. They enjoy walking the boundary line, getting a shot in at the boss, pushing the rules to the limit, or daring you to knock that chip off their shoulder. They enjoy the role of outsider, a sort of Clint Eastwood of the organization. Although the team needs people who will speak out with integrity about important issues, they do not need members who simply enjoy being disagreeable. Ineffective Challengers use the cloak of honesty to further their personal agendas. But in the final analysis, *their* actions are dishonest. Most important, they often divide the team and create unnecessary delays caused by the confrontations. In the end, the Challenger who goes over the boundary of effective behavior becomes, at best, an annoyance— a person to be tolerated.

One especially ineffective Challenger was a member of an advisory board of a nonprofit community agency. He said that he represented the underclass of the city and that the agency was not doing enough to help this group. Although some of his objections to their programs were helpful, other board members did not consider them because (1) he seemed to oppose everything the agency did and (2) his manner was abrasive and included personal attacks on the staff. The more his points were ignored, the more confrontational and self-righteous he became. In the end, he became the "crazy radical" whom no one took seriously.

The Ineffective Challenger: A Checklist of Adjectives

1. Rigid
2. Arrogant
3. Self-righteous
4. Aggressive
5. Unyielding

Dealing with the Ineffective Team Player When It Is You

For individuals, awareness is the first step to behavioral change. It is important that we understand our team player style and the potential that exists for ineffectiveness. Self-understanding and self-assessment can tell us our primary team player style. Then we can use this information to become sensitive to the possibilities of overusing our strengths to the point of ineffectiveness. Contributors can pull back when they become too technical, Collaborators can stop when they overemphasize strategic issues, Communicators can put on the brakes when they get mired in group process, and Challengers can call a halt when opposition becomes an end in itself. Self-knowledge can help develop an appreciation of other team player styles and, therefore, tolerance of different approaches to effective team play.

Self-understanding can be supplemented by the use of a self-assessment instrument. The *Parker Team Player Survey* (see Resource C) can give you a reading of your team player style and potential weaknesses as a team player. The instrument is a form of self-feedback, as it measures your perception of yourself. The results can lead to an acknowledgment of your strengths and a plan for improvement. The plan should include (1) learning ways to make better use of your strong points, (2) cutting back on the overuse of your style, (3) using strategies for incorporating behaviors from some of the other styles, and (4) developing an appreciation of people who help the team in different ways.

An alternative is to obtain feedback from other team members who have had an opportunity to observe you as a team player. You can ask for the feedback informally in a conversation, or you can use a structured feedback process facilitated by the use of the *Parker Team Player Survey: Styles of Another Person* completed by other team members.[1]

Dealing with the Ineffective Team Player When It Is Someone Else

The following guidelines will be especially useful for the team leader, but they are applicable to all team members who observe counterproductive team players.

Listen. Maybe, just maybe, the person has a point. Often what you perceive as ineffective team play is simply your inability to appreciate a person with another style. In these situations, his or her primary style may be your least active style, and vice versa. What you see as obstructionist may actually be effective challenging of a team decision. What you see as pie-in-the-sky thinking may actually be long-term goal setting. Listen, and use your paraphrasing, questioning, and summarizing skills before moving forward on the assumption that the person's behavior is not helpful.

Meet Privately. Ask the person questions such as: "Why are you on this team?" "What do you see as your role?" "What concerns do you have about the way the team is going?" Probe to uncover the causes of resistance. It may be that he or she is experiencing a personal or family crisis and that this team responsibility comes at a bad time. It may be that this person is also on three other teams and having great difficulty prioritizing all the work. It may be that language differences are preventing the person from understanding and participating in the discussions. It may be that the team member's style is in a distinct minority on the team, so he or she feels out of place. For example, a Communicator found herself on a team that had no interest in the process aspects of the team's operation. Unable to confront the team with her concerns, she sat silently through the meetings. The purpose of the private meeting is to uncover the needs of a person in this kind of situation and to determine if those needs can be satisfied on this team.

Reestablish Team Norms. Reestablishing team norms is recommended when there are several ineffective team players, because it uses group process to deal with them. If your team has been in existence for some time, it may be necessary to bring out the list again and use it to remind the group of their agreements. If your team does not have a set of norms, someone (usually the leader) should facilitate a discussion of team member expectations, with the goal of developing a list of acceptable behaviors. You are looking for expectations in areas such as completing work assignments, attendance, starting and ending on time, participation in discussions, raising objections, format for presentations, decision making, and confronting differences. Team norms have two functions: they provide (1) a guide for self-monitoring by team members, and (2) a basis for the team leader or member to give feedback to another member who has violated a norm. Often a discussion that centers on developing a set of team norms will lead to an assessment of the extent to which the norms currently are being followed.

Negotiate. Stated simply, negotiation involves an agreement in which I agree to do something if you agree to do something. For example, if you agree to back off from your insistence that we clarify team-member roles until we get an agreement on our mission statement, I will let you lead a discussion on roles at the beginning of our next meeting. Negotiation often neutralizes a situation for the moment, but it may not eliminate the problem unless the negotiation leads to a permanent agreement on new behavior. For example, "I will allow a full consideration of the ethical aspects of product research if you agree to support fully all team decisions reached by consensus."

Positive Reinforcement. If the person does make a useful contribution, however small, try to make him or her feel good about that acceptable behavior. Reinforcement can send a message that this is the desired behavior. At a recent meeting, a team player who rarely spoke said, "What is the point of all this?" The leader responded, "That's a good question. How does this specific task fit into our overall project plan?" The team leader's response did two things: (1) it helped the individual team player, and (2) it helped the team focus on the need to see beyond the immediate tasks to the big picture.

Contact the Person's Boss. Sometimes your best efforts at listening, meeting, processing, negotiating, and reinforcing just do not work. You must go to the person's boss and discuss the problem. The boss may be able to provide some insight into the team player's behavior, make a suggestion on how to handle the person, or offer to talk to the person directly. In one recent case, the boss acknowledged that this was an inappropriate assignment and agreed to remove the person from the team.

Confront the Person. Confrontation really means confronting the behavior exhibited by the person. This is best done privately. But sometimes privacy is not possible, and direct feedback during the meeting is necessary. You must be specific and point to the person's behavior that is inhibiting the team. You may elect to discuss how the behavior is affecting you. For example, "Stan, your insistence that we collect more data is slowing us down, causing us to miss deadlines and to renege on commitments to clients. Frankly, I'm frustrated because we have vigorously followed the project plan that you agreed to, yet you still do not seem to be satisfied."

Say Farewell. Some people must go. Some people just cannot be rehabilitated. They must be transferred, reassigned, or simply fired.

Notes

1. Available from www.cpp.com.

5

TEAM PLAYERS
AS TEAM LEADERS

It almost goes without saying, but let's say it anyway: the leader is critical to the success of a team. Our view of leadership has been changed dramatically in the past few years by Bennis (1988), Bennis and Nanus (1985), Block (1987), and Kouzes and Posner (1987). Leaders are people who create an inspired vision for the organization, communicate a sense of enthusiasm for the effort, and are honest and authentic in their interactions with people. But team leaders must also be effective managers (Wilson, George, Wellins, and Byham, 1994; Zenger, Musselwhite, Horson, and Perrin, 1994; Hackman, 2002). They need to see both the forest and the trees. Teams need to look ahead and to produce a quality product today. A team of programmers, for example, needs to consider the future possibilities of computing technology as well as to meet next month's deadline for the release of a new system. The human resources team needs to have a plan for the work force in the year 2010 while they get set to launch a series of seminars on business ethics next quarter. However, the world of teams has changed in many important ways, making the job of team leader much more difficult than it was in the 1990s. The team leader must adapt to a variety of new challenges posed by

- The increasing use of cross-functional teams, whereby team members effectively report to a functional manager rather than the team leader

- The growth of global teams populated with people from many countries representing a variety of cultures, many of whom may have limited experience in working together

- The widespread use of technology-based meeting tools such as teleconference, video conference, and web conference, and the corresponding lack of opportunities for face-to-face inter- actions with teammates

- The phenomenon of subject matter experts serving on multiple teams, resulting in divided loyalties, conflicting priorities, and competing time pressures

- The increasing tendency of senior management to hold the team leader accountable for the success of the team, coupled with overall rising expectations for team success by these same managers

- New pressures from team members for rewards and recogni- tion for their participation on these teams, with so much of their workday spent in team meetings, preparing for team meetings, and completing tasks for a team

The effective team leader is an effective team player. Effective team leadership requires the articulation of a vision; the creation of a clear mission; and the development of goals, objectives, and action plans. The most effective leaders involve team members in these activities. Effective team leaders ensure the completion of immediate tasks and work assignments in a high-quality and timely fashion. The most effective leaders inspire a desire to produce quality products and ser- vices and to provide excellent customer service. They have the abil- ity to communicate with team members around the world and with important players outside the team. The most effective leaders have excellent skills in listening, conflict resolution, consensus building, and meeting management, including the new technologies such as web conferencing. And they create an open environment in which members feel free to express their views with candor and integrity. The most effective leaders are challengers of the status quo and are supportive of others who push for risk taking and innovation.

A team player can be either a member or a leader. Many people play both roles in an organization and, in fact, may play both roles during the same day. In the morning, you attend the division staff meeting with the vice president as team leader. In the afternoon, you facilitate a new product project team meeting in which you serve as team leader.

Your team player style remains consistent as you make your transition from member to leader and back again. However, the style may manifest itself in different ways depending on expectations of the role.

As a member, the Contributor can be depended on to provide accurate data in support of the team's effort, and as a leader, the Contributor structures the operations of the team to solve technical problems efficiently. In a leadership role, the Collaborator tends to be a strategic thinker, and as a member, the Collaborator does what is required to keep the team moving toward its goals. Communicators as team leaders are noted for their participative management approach, and as members, they encourage and support the involvement of others through the use of their communication style. As a member, the Challenger raises questions about team issues and sometimes questions the leader; as the team leader, the Challenger encourages the norm of candor and openness to ensure that the team looks at all sides of an issue.

In the final analysis, the style remains consistent as the roles change. As the roles change, the expectations of the person in the role vary. Leaders are expected to behave differently from members, and they do. The behavior, however, is consistent with the team player style. In the following sections, we will review how each style of team player carries out five important leadership functions.

The Contributor as Leader

The Contributor sees the team as a vehicle to solve business problems, with an emphasis on efficiency. The Contributor is guided by the philosophy "If it ain't broke, don't fix it." The most effective Contributor leaders are effective managers. They get things done and they get them done well. In addition, "they fine-tune the structure of the team so that it fosters rather than impedes teamwork" (Hackman, 2002, p. 205).

Planning tends to be tactical in approach. The Contributor emphasizes short-term, specific, measurable objectives with detailed action plans. The planning process is data-based, with a heavy use of demographic statistics, reports of past results, and business forecasts.

Communication tends to be economical. The Contributor is often a person of few words. Contributors do not waste time engaging in small talk (unless the culture requires it) because they like to get to the point and then get on with the work. In other words, Contributors do not see communication as work. They prefer written communication (especially email) over oral communication. Presentations tend to be formal speeches with lots of overhead transparencies buttressed by detailed handouts. The Contributor usually prefers meetings that make use of teleconferencing, video conferencing, and web conferencing. When there is a document to edit, the Contributor will look to a program that allows people on the network to annotate the document, with limited verbal communication.

Risk taking tends to be conservative. The Contributor prefers well-researched, well-reasoned proposals. Change, in the view of the Contributor, is an incremental process backed up by a detailed plan. In a given period, risks should be limited in number. As a leader, the Contributor will push the team to make the existing system work better before trying new ventures.

Problem solving tends to be analytical. As a team leader, the Contributor provides the team with a structured model involving a step-by-step plan. Problem solving, as viewed by the Contributor, requires a careful assessment of data, use of technical expertise, and rigorous examination of costs and benefits.

Decision making tends to favor decisions that are practical, logical, and cost-effective. The Contributor ensures that the team's decisions are consistent with company policies and procedures and are in the mainstream of the corporate culture. As the team's leader, the Contributor expects decisions to be based on clear evidence, with the outcome well documented for the record.

The Contributor Leader: The Downside

As a leader, the Contributor can be too practical, too conservative, and overly task oriented. Contributors can be so obsessed with *efficiency* that they forget about *effectiveness*. Meetings become something to get through ("so we can get back to work") rather than an important opportunity for interaction among members, discussions of key decisions, and assessments of team progress. Viewed from the outside, team meetings may lack energy, enthusiasm, and warmth. They sometimes look rather dull and boring. The Contributor as leader will often fail to recognize cultural differences on the team and their impact on communication and decision making. The importance of process and team building, including the development of norms, may not be considered.

Leaders who are also subject matter experts with narrow technical specialties seem to be most prone to becoming ineffective Contributor leaders. They covet the leadership position for the status and salary increase but dislike the interpersonal responsibilities that go with it, and they often lack the vision to see beyond the immediate technical problem facing the team. As leaders of functional work teams, they often spend lots of time looking over the shoulders of team members; in the extreme, they step in and take over the problems.

The Contributor leader focuses the team on detailed problem solving but loses sight of member needs for inclusion, responsibility, and recognition. They also lose sight of the big picture—how the work of the team fits into the organization's goals and priorities.

The Collaborator as Leader

In a leadership role, the Collaborator might be described as a "shirtsleeve visionary." The Collaborator sees the leader's role as providing a view of the future—focus, mission, goals, or, as

Hackman (2002) put it, "a compelling direction" (p. 205). At the same time, he or she is ready to pitch in and help out as required. The Collaborator approaches the key leadership functions with a particular style.

Planning tends to be strategic. The planning process emphasizes long-term goals backed up by action plans that involve all team members. As a leader, the Collaborator will present these goals, including the expectations of senior management and the new global marketplace, but will encourage member involvement and will be open to all views of the team's future. However, the team's goals must be consistent with the overall corporate plan and the expectations of senior management.

Communication tends to focus on big-picture issues. The Collaborator may lack patience for detailed technical or scientific discussions. As a leader, he or she likes a lot of discussion on organizational direction and will regularly ask for input. The Collaborator is effective at managing the outside—communicating with other key stakeholders both within and outside the organization. The telephone is the preferred communication medium, although Collaborators are often well-known for periodic emails on strategic direction.

Risk taking tends to focus on the potential gain of a given risk rather than the potential loss. As leaders, Collaborators are willing to take planned risks because they are confident they will be able to deal with unanticipated problems. Although they believe "nothing ventured, nothing gained," they calculate all risks for their contribution to the team's mission and goals. Collaborators are known to take risks that stretch organizational policies and procedures in order to help the team achieve its goals. Their motto is "It is easier to get forgiveness than permission."

Problem solving tends to put all problems in some larger context. As a leader, the Collaborator looks for the implications of a problem and the impact of potential solutions on organizational effectiveness. Collaborators are often willing to pitch in and help out where necessary, to obtain the necessary resources for the team, and to ensure that the appropriate team members are recognized for solving the problem.

Decision making tends to look at both sides of an issue and favor an open process. However, as a leader, the Collaborator wants all team decisions tied to the long-term strategy. Collaborators value commitment to all team decisions, and they work hard to ensure that everyone is willing to put his or her shoulder to the wheel. They will insist that the team revisit key decisions to assess results.

The Collaborator Leader: The Downside

As a leader, the Collaborator can become too global and overly ambitious and can place too much emphasis on the long-term aspects of the team's mission. The Collaborator wants so badly to be a visionary and forward-looking leader that he or she loses sight of the work required to get to the future. The Collaborator may lack patience with interpersonal issues, including the need to understand and appreciate cultural differences among team members.

The Collaborator leader's enthusiasm for a strategic approach to team activities can be misplaced. I am familiar with a team leader who is too far out in front of the rest of the team. His push for strategic plans has not been well received by other team members because they feel the organization is currently poorly managed. Their view is that quality and customer service need to be significantly improved before any new ideas should be explored. The net result of this lack of consensus is tension, poor communication, and ineffective coordination.

The Collaborator leader who succeeds in putting shared visions and goals into place will often fail to manage the process. In one organization, a team spent two days in an off-site meeting developing a set of long-term goals. Six months later, these were still on flip-chart paper, rolled up in a corner of the plant manager's office. This may be an extreme case (or is it?), because there is usually follow-up at least to the extent that the products of a planning meeting are printed and distributed to all team members. The ineffective Collaborator leader does not like to manage the real follow-up that involves monitoring progress, allocating resources, revising plans, and coordinating individual efforts. He or she also may not push hard for internal system changes such as incorporating team player performance in the overall employee performance management process as well as team rewards and individual team member recognition.

The Communicator as Leader

In leadership roles, Communicators are highly participatory. They value a positive work climate, enjoy a family atmosphere, and believe a team that works well together is more effective. In carrying out the key leadership functions, Communicators pay particular attention to group process issues.

Planning tends to give heavy emphasis to the involvement of all team members in the development of the plan. For the Communicator, the process by which the plan is prepared is as important as the content of the plan. Communicators like to make sure that the plan is acceptable to everyone or at least that everyone has an opportunity to influence its direction. They may also initiate a process designed to create a team rewards and recognition program.

Communication tends to be warm, relaxed, and generally enjoyable. As team leaders, Communicators make special efforts to have enjoyable team meetings. They realize that many people hate meetings and, therefore, will make sure the room is comfortable, have coffee served, chat with people prior to the meeting, use humor to break the ice, and use other climate-setting techniques. They will make a special effort to be the first one on the line for a teleconference in order to greet each person as they enter the meeting, to begin with some informal conversation, and then to ensure that each person has an opportunity to comment on key agenda items. The Communicator is a good listener and is especially effective at informal one-on-one meetings with other members.

Risk taking tends toward risks that will improve the internal functioning of the team. The Communicator as team leader will want to explore fully the impact of a proposed action on the team climate and to ensure that all members are aware of the possible consequences. A risk for the Communicator would be to give negative feedback to a member of the team.

Problem solving tends to favor high-involvement problem-solving approaches. As a team leader, the Communicator is able to communicate a sense of urgency and, if necessary, enthusiasm for a problem and the need to solve it. The Communicator believes strongly that people who are closest to the problem should be deeply involved in the development of the solution. The Communicator leader will try to facilitate an effective resolution of differences among members with varying opinions.

Decision making tends to be participative. The Communicator in a leadership role likes to make sure all views have been heard before making a decision. On major decisions, he or she favors the consensus method. Participative decision making works well when it is supported at the top. At H-E-B Grocery's milk plant in San Antonio, Texas, the vice president of manufacturing says that "our strongest team leaders are those that make the *fewest* decisions on their teams because the teams are empowered and capable and very much involved in the decisions that affect their business" (Dudlicek, 2003, p. 30). The Communicator will resist all efforts to refer decisions to a higher authority but rather will try to facilitate a decision at the team level.

The Communicator Leader: The Downside

As a team leader, the Communicator can become obsessed with process and see interpersonal communication as the panacea for all team problems. He or she can emphasize climate setting to the point where team goals and the completion of work assignments are incidental to a "don't' worry, be happy" attitude. Even more destructive to the team is the development of norms that discourage internal criticism. The Communicator leader who is overly concerned with climate often discourages, smothers, or in other ways inhibits well-intentioned questioning of the team's work.

Leaders of teams in voluntary organizations and professional associations are especially prone to these excesses. Combine human resource–development or organization-development specialists together in a professional society, and you get strong potential for an obsessive concern for good feelings, sometimes to the exclusion of making hard but important choices.

Beware, too, of recent converts—leaders who receive feedback that they are too task oriented and, with a vengeance, try to become Communicators overnight. They take so much time and put so much effort into their process skills that they forget the team has a job to do.

The Challenger as Leader

As a team leader, the Challenger is no longer questioning authority (unless it is a higher authority) but is attempting to set a team norm of openness and candor. He or she wants all team members to have questions about the team's mission and methods and, in a leadership role, will continue to use a questioning mode in regard to reports, presentations, and overall team strategy. The Challenger has a unique approach to the key leadership functions.

Planning tends to be oriented toward pushing the team to consider new directions. The Challenger favors the use of brainstorming and other free-form planning techniques. He or she encourages the team to set aside self-limiting thinking—"it's not in the budget," "we tried that last year"—and to seek out new areas for change and growth. The Challenger does not worry if the plan goes against the grain; he or she pushes the team to set "stretch" objectives that go beyond the safe and predictable.

Communication tends to be open, direct, and, yes, challenging. As a team leader, the Challenger likes to *quickly* get to the point.

He or she uses questions to make points ("What do you think we should do to deal with the problem of . . .?") and to bring out information ("Can you provide us with . . .?"). Challengers like meetings as learning vehicles because they enjoy the give-and-take of discussion and debate.

Risk taking tends to focus on the potential gain from every proposed team risk. As a leader, the Challenger is action oriented and likes to push the team to new frontiers. The Challenger has a high tolerance for uncertainty and failure but rarely talks about the possibility of failing. He or she encourages innovation and allows members the freedom to fail, because "good tries" are not punished. A Challenger is likely to say, "A mistake is just another way of doing something."

Problem solving tends to be unstructured. As a leader, the Challenger will push hard for identification of the real problem by peeling away the symptoms. He or she will raise tough questions about the problem analysis—especially about the data used to support the conclusions. The Challenger wants the team to develop many alternative solutions and, again, will insist that each alternative undergo careful scrutiny by the members.

Decision making tends to favor decisions that are "right," ethical, and, of course, legal. As the leader, the Challenger will weigh the facts and then encourage the team to use their experience to reach a conclusion. The Challenger talks a great deal about "gut decisions" and "judgment calls." He or she will also push to uncover hidden resistance on the part of team members and will encourage members to have all concerns addressed by the team before reaching a decision.

The Challenger Leader: The Downside

As leaders, Challengers can be too extreme in their positions, can waste resources on ill-conceived risks, and can offend others with their confrontational manner. They may push the team to develop projects that are presented as innovative but that lack solid data and careful analysis. Or they may promote projects that are well outside the current strategy of the organization. Ineffective Challenger leaders will often establish a tense climate in team meetings because they debate every issue and argue with team members. If a leader is a technical "guru," members will often be afraid to make presentations or offer opinions, as they fear being "shot down" by the leader. This type of negative climate can be especially destructive if the team is global and the membership is culturally diverse. Some members—those who are not comfortable with confrontation or public criticism—may shrink from participation and fail to offer their opinion and share their expertise.

The team's image with key stakeholders can be adversely affected by a contentious Challenger leader. If the leader is the principal point of contact, he or she may offend important people (such as senior management or government regulatory agencies) in positions to help the team with budget, staff, and access. One extremely bright and creative team leader in a nonprofit agency was simply too confrontational in his interpersonal communication with key players from various funding sources. He saw them as dull and reactionary. They saw him as offensive. His ineffective style blocked people from seeing his many talents, and in the end the agency lost many opportunities for additional projects that could have been financed by grants from government agencies and private foundations.

Personal-Development Planning for Team Leaders

As a team leader you may find it useful to identify your team player style and to assess its effectiveness in the context of the needs of the team. The analysis of the impact of your style on the team can lead to a plan for improvement. The team may require a style of leadership that you are not providing. For example, a team in one of my client companies was extremely effective in delivering on its short-term commitments. The leader, an effective Contributor, was able to design and manage a production control system. She was also able to see the value of thinking strategically about future needs in technology and human resource development. In effect, she began to use some of the strengths of the Collaborator style. In another case, the leader of a user-developer problem-solving team was effective at getting the members to air their differences in a "civilized" fashion, but the net result was that people were being too polite. Following some feedback from me, she was able to move from the Communicator mode to use more of her Challenger strengths. The team needed more candor and openness as they looked at new systems, so she modeled and encouraged this behavior.

Successful Team-Building Strategies for Team Leaders

The most successful team leaders fuse the strengths of all four styles to create an effective team. Let's assume that you have been appointed leader of a start-up team or that you have assumed leadership of an existing team.

Get to Know the Team. Prior to any team activities, meet each team player informally. Share something of your background and experience as well as your feelings about this team. Try to find out each member's interests and possible concerns about the work of the team. If he or she has a particular motivation, see if that need can be met by participation on the team. The skills of the Communicator will be especially helpful here.

Define the Team's Purpose. Tell the team what you know about management's expectations for the team, including time-table, budget, and constraints. Answer questions openly and look to address common concerns about the team's future. Engage the members in a discussion leading to clear goals and a project plan. The goal-setting strengths of the Collaborator will be useful here.

Clarify Roles. Eliminate problems down the road by an early discussion of what is expected of each team player. On one cross-functional team, everyone was expected to brief his or her department about team progress, the leader was expected to deal with senior management, and others had responsibility for interfacing with specific stakeholders. The unpleasant work of taking minutes, setting up the meeting room, and preparing reports was rotated among team members. Role clarification is often the concern of both the Collaborator and the Contributor.

Establish Norms. Early in the life of the team, the Communicator will encourage the team to develop a list of norms or standards of behavior for team members. Whereas roles establish expectations, norms provide members with guidelines on how to work together. Here is a partial list of norms generated at the first meeting of a task force expected to have a six-month life:

As a member of this team I will

- Honor my commitments to the team
- In disagreeing with my teammates, focus on the issues and not engage in personal attacks
- Show up or call in on time for all team meetings
- Inform the team leader if I am unable to attend a meeting
- Support and work to implement all team decisions once a consensus has been reached
- Communicate team decisions and actions to my management in a timely manner
- Offer to pitch in and help out my teammates
- Maintain the confidentiality of all team discussions

Draw Up a Game Plan. Mission and goals begin the planning process. Effective leaders insist that the team prepare objectives and action plans to ensure success in achieving the mission and realizing the goals. The plan also lets everyone know his or her assignments and due dates. The plan is a management tool for the leader to use in assessing progress, allocating resources, and preparing reports. The task strengths of the Contributor will be useful here.

Encourage Questions. The norm of *civilized disagreement* should be mandatory for all teams. The team leader is critical to the establishment of a climate that supports the expression of differences. Demonstrate your willingness to question the status quo, and be open to comments that overtly disagree with your position. The most powerful motivator of team-member behavior is the modeling of that behavior by the team leader; almost as powerful are support and encouragement from the leader. The Challenger's strengths are appropriate here.

Share the Limelight. The Communicator is usually the person who will remember to give recognition to individual team player contributions and acknowledge team results. When opportunities for external recognition arise, spread the light around. Whether it is a presentation to senior management, an article in a company publication, or a picture in the local newspaper, give everyone a chance for recognition. On a cross-functional team, provide functional managers with feedback on team members for inclusion in the member's performance appraisal.

Be Participatory. Involve as many team members as possible in the work of the team. Spread around the work assignments as much as you can—especially the ones that mean positive exposure (making a presentation) and ones that are not much fun (collating the handouts). When important decisions arise or key problems must be solved, use the consensus method. A consensus decision requires involvement and usually results in a better outcome. The tools of the Communicator will be helpful.

Celebrate Accomplishments. The best teams work hard and play hard. As a team leader, you should encourage the team to plan celebrations to mark milestones, product launches, meeting of quotas, and other significant events. If the organization does not have a program of team rewards, you should make it a team activity. Again, the Communicator is often the person who will plan the party.

Assess Team Effectiveness. Teams, like individuals, periodically need to take stock—to have a check-up, much like an annual health examination. As a leader, you should be the person to initiate this process. If you have just assumed leadership, this would be a good time to engage the team in a systematic review. And then, at least once a year, the team should ask and answer some basic questions:

- What are our strengths?
- What elements of our goals and project plan need revision?
- How are we progressing toward our goals?
- How effective are team meetings?
- How well do we work with important stakeholders?
- Is there clarity about team member roles?
- Are we satisfied with the quality of our work?
- How do our customers feel about us?
- What changes do we need to make?
- Is it still fun?

The *Parker Team-Development Survey* in Resource A may produce other ideas for a team assessment. The strengths of all four styles should be useful here.

Table 5.1 presents a summary of how each team player carries out the five important leadership functions discussed in this chapter.

Table 5.1 The Team Player as Leader

Style/Function	Contributor	Collaborator	Communicator	Challenger
Planning	Tactical	Strategic	Total involvement	Likes new directions
	Statistical	Visionary	Wide acceptance	Pushes for "stretch"
	Specific	Open	Agreement on process	objectives
	Measurable	Big picture		
	Conservative	Involving		
Communication	Economical	General	Warm and friendly	Open
	Written	Verbal	Informal	Candid
	Formal	Uses telephone	Uses humor	Confrontational
	To the point	Unstructured	Emphasizes comfort	Questioning
	Detailed	Organizational	Listens	Prefers meetings
Risk Taking	Conservative	Liberal	Explores impact on team process	Focuses on potentials
	Incremental	Open to all ideas	Favors process risks	Pushes the frontiers
	Planner	Goal directed	Discusses consequences of risks	Encourages innovation
	Pilot tested	Accepts risks	Gives feedback	Supports "good tries"
	Researched	Planner		

(continued)

Table 5.1 (Continued)

Style/Function	Contributor	Collaborator	Communicator	Challenger
Problem Solving	Analytical	Looks for context	Favors involvement	Unstructured
	Structured	Looks for implications	Emphasizes process	Looks for "real" problem
	Data based	Pitches in	Facilitates conflicts	Questions analysis
	Technical	Gives credit	Favors hands-on solutions	Examines data
	Rigorous	Gets resources		Costs versus benefits
Decision Making	Logical	Open to both sides	Participative	Legal
	Mainstream	Consistent with goals	Uses consensus	Ethical "Right"
	Cost-effective	Looks for commitment	Resists leader control	Probes for resistance
	Practical	Revisits decisions		
	Consistent	Wants involvement		

6

ADAPTIVE TEAM PLAYERS

Much like individuals, teams experience stages of development. Teams mature from early formation through various phases into a developed organization—provided certain positive actions are taken. Again like individuals, teams also can get stuck in an immature phase and can suffer a case of arrested growth and ineffectiveness. Team players have an important role to play in each stage. Effective team players can successfully move a team toward maturity with specific, positive actions.

Tuckman (1965) identified four stages of team development:

1. Forming
2. Storming
3. Norming
4. Performing

In the *forming* stage, team members test the waters to determine what type of behavior will be acceptable, the nature of the team's task, and how the group will be used to get the work done. Forming is a period of dependency during which members look to the leader, to management, or to some existing rules for guidance. Tuckman compared this stage to that period of orientation and dependency experienced by infants and very young children.

The second stage, characterized by conflict among team members and resistance to the task, is *storming*. Storming is characterized by hostility among team members and toward the leader as members resist the structure of the group. Similarly, there is some resistance to the team's task—although the nature of the resistance will vary with the type of task. For example, an impersonal technical task will not evoke as much emotionality as will a team-building exercise. Often the leader's style will prevent the conflict of the storming stage from surfacing in a natural fashion. As a result, the resistance will emerge in unproductive ways (for example, in members not living up to commitments). Tuckman compared the storming of a team to the rebelliousness of a young child toward parental and school controls.

A sense of group cohesion develops in the third stage. This *norming* stage is characterized by acceptance of the team, a willingness to make it work, and the development of team norms—standards of behavior that the team develops for guiding member interaction and for dealing with the task. Information is freely shared and acted on, and openness and trust emerge among team members. This team development stage is comparable to the socialization phase associated with child development.

As interpersonal relationships become stabilized and as roles are clarified, the team moves into the fourth and final stage, *performing*. The group has a structure, purpose, and clear roles and is ready to tackle the task. The emphasis here is on results, as positive problem solving and decision making take place. With interpersonal problems in the past and a focus on the real problems of life, this stage is compared to the mature phase in human development.

Tuckman's four stages of team development are a model—a convenient way of analyzing a team and the role of team players during each stage. The model is a tool—not a consistent picture of the real world. The real history of organizational teams can be a bit messier. Some teams begin by storming and then revert to the goal setting usually associated with the forming phase. At the same meeting, some members will act as if they have reached an agreement on norms while a few are still shouting each other down.

Team players should look for the dominant theme of the team—a theme that reflects the stage of development. Once you identify the stage, a quick assessment should reveal the team's needs and your role in helping the team successfully negotiate its way to maturity.

Forming

This first stage focuses primarily on the start-up of a new team. The same dynamics may occur when a new leader takes over a team, when there is a significant change in team composition, or when the team's purpose is altered. In effect, there is a re-formation.

During the forming stage, there is a lack of clarity about the purpose of the group and about the expectations of the members. Members do not know each other, so they tend to be polite and obedient. Typically, they want to be told what to do, member status is based on their outside roles, and interactions and discussions are superficial and tend to be directed to the formal leader.

Contributor. At this stage, the Contributor wants to know what his or her role will be on the team. At the same time, there is a strong concern about expectations: What will I be expected to do? How much time will this take? Which of my skills will be needed? What specific tasks will I be responsible for?

As a Contributor, here is how you can help:

1. Initiate a discussion of possible team tasks.
2. Suggest that team members contribute information or opinions on the issue, based on their area of expertise.
3. Offer to study an aspect of the problem and report at the next meeting; suggest that other team members do the same.
4. Ask the leader to provide suggestions on team procedures (for example, frequency of meetings, length, location, minutes, and agenda). If you are the leader, make sure these topics are on the agenda for the first meeting.

Collaborator. The Collaborator wants to know the mission or goal of the team. Although Collaborators may have some ideas about the team's direction, they usually wait for the leader to define the purpose.

If you are a Collaborator, you can help in the following ways:

1. Ask the leader to provide his or her view of the team's purpose. If you are the leader, structure a discussion designed to create a team mission. Share your views with the team.
2. Offer your opinion on the mission of the team.
3. Encourage other team members to provide their views of the mission.
4. Suggest that the team develop goals and objectives that support the mission.
5. Share with the team what you know about management's expectations for the team, including such areas as outcomes, timeline, budget, and priority.

Communicator. As the team is forming, Communicators want to know "who has been invited to the party." They have a need to make personal contact with other team members. Concerns include these: Who are these people? Will they accept me? What resources do they bring to the team?

During the forming stage, you as a Communicator can do several things to help:

1. Introduce yourself to as many people as possible prior to the meeting.
2. Ask the leader to explain how the team membership was selected. If you are the leader, speak with each person prior to the first meeting or discuss it at the first meeting.
3. Suggest a brief introductory activity that includes all members offering information about how they spend their time outside of work, such as hobbies and interests.
4. On a cross-functional team, suggest that the team create a "talent bank" listing each person's areas of expertise.

5. On a global team, try to determine if language and cultural differences may impact member participation.

Challenger. Challengers begin with a skeptical view of the team. They see it as "another do-nothing committee" or "more meetings that take me away from my real job." The Challenger wants to be sure the team will accomplish something useful and that the group will deal openly and honestly with issues.

As a Challenger, you can be useful to the team in the following ways:

1. Ask the group if they are satisfied with the team's mission and goals.
2. Openly express your reservations about the team's purpose or methods.
3. Raise questions for the leader. If you are the leader, encourage members to ask questions, and when a member does ask a question, be sure to maintain a nonjudgmental attitude. If possible, meet with each person privately and try to answer his or her questions.
4. Suggest an exercise that asks each team member to express concerns about the team's charter, goals, methods, membership, and management's expectations for the team.
5. On a cross-functional team, initiate a discussion that focuses on limitations, such as conflicting priorities, that members may need to share with the team.

Storming

The initial reluctance to express opinions is followed by a period of disagreement. Members feel free to disagree with each other and with the leader. Some of the questions, concerns, and even frustrations that people brought with them are now expressed. Ideas are challenged, closely evaluated, and sometimes shot down. Members form alliances, resulting in subgroup conflict; questions arise about both the task and process of the team; and there is some task avoidance as members enjoy the arguments.

Some teams never go through this stage because they are fearful that the expression of differences will tear the team apart. However, the conflict need not be heated or counterproductive. Quite the contrary; teams that fail to experience storming never learn how to deal with differences. As a result, they develop a form of passive resistance whereby members simply go along with the leader or a small cadre of members, even though they are not really in agreement. They may even express their disagreement by engaging in dysfunctional behavior such as coming late to meetings or failing to honor commitments. Teams that have not successfully passed through the storming phase tend to be more divided and less creative.

Contributor. Contributors are concerned that this stage will result in a failure to get the basic job done. They wonder whether all this heat will ultimately shed any real light on the subject. The Contributor is concerned about the need to conduct an objective, factual examination of the team problem rather than just presenting opposing opinions.

During the storming stage, as a Contributor you should do the following:

1. Remain objective and encourage other team members to look at both sides of all issues.
2. Ask people for data to support their opinions.
3. Remind the team of the need to complete their action items.
4. Suggest that the team remain focused on the specific work that needs to be done.

Collaborator. During storming, the Collaborator is concerned about the team's need to see the big picture. He or she wonders whether these conflicts will detract from team efforts to move forward, in a coordinated fashion, toward the goals. The Collaborator does not want to see team differences result in failure to pitch in and help each other out. In the final analysis, the Collaborator worries that team conflicts will dilute member commitment to the overall team purpose.

The team can benefit from the Collaborator who will

1. Be open to ideas and encourage others to do the same.
2. Ask how opinions expressed affect the team's mission and goals.
3. Be prepared to revise the mission and goals based on opinions and data.
4. Be willing to help out other team members.
5. Remind the team about management's expectations for the team.

Communicator. Among the four styles, the Communicator feels most comfortable and potentially has the most to contribute during the storming stage. Communicators understand that conflict among members is useful as long as it is expressed in a positive manner. They want to be sure that the team establishes effective norms regarding the expression of opinions and the resolution of differences, and they are concerned that members listen to each other, discuss the merits of the issue, and not engage in personal attacks.

At this stage, you as a Communicator can help the team in several ways:

1. Model good listening skills (for example, paraphrasing), and encourage others to do the same.
2. Suggest norms for resolving differences.
3. Involve quiet members in discussion.
4. Encourage the leader to ensure that all sides are heard and, if no agreement is possible, to make a decision. If you are the

leader, enforce norms regarding positive communication and conflict resolution.

5. Be aware that people from certain cultures are not comfortable with open conflict and will not readily disagree with another member, especially the leader, in a meeting.

Challenger. Challengers are likely to be key players during the storming stage. They will test the team and the leader on issues of task and process, and they want to know whether the team will be receptive to tough questions that go to the core of the team's mission and goals. At this point, the Challenger will push the team to explore the limits of their mandate and to consider the innovative aspects of their problem.

As a Challenger, you can be useful to the team in the following ways:

1. Model positive assertive behavior (for example, challenge the issue, not the person).

2. Be willing to back off when a clear consensus emerges.

3. Acknowledge the team leader and other members when they listen to your ideas.

4. Encourage the team to take well-conceived risks and innovative approaches to the team's task as well as to its own internal processes such as rewards and recognition.

5. Recognize that your confrontational style may not be well received by introverts on the team or members from some other cultures.

Norming

As teams emerge from the storming phase, they learn from their successful experience in dealing with each other. The team establishes guidelines for conflict resolution, decision making, interpersonal communication, assignment completion, and meeting management. Shared leadership becomes more apparent.

The embedding of these norms also leads to an increase in trust. It becomes possible to disagree with each other without the conflict leading to a personal attack. Members begin to enjoy the meetings and each other. A competitive cohesion develops as the team feels superior to other teams, and there is the laughing and joking that is associated with the informality of effective teams. But behind the surface of all these positive elements lurks the potential for groupthink (Janus, 1972), whereby a competitive and informal climate can inhibit members from willingly challenging the prevailing thinking.

Contributor. The Contributor has an important role to play at this stage as task accomplishment goes forward. With positive norms established, the team is positioned to get on with the work. However, with the potential for groupthink, the Contributor is concerned that standards may be compromised and lower quality accepted.

To assist the team during the norming stage, you as a Contributor should do the following:

1. Insist on high quality standards for all team output.
2. Help the team make effective use of all the resources at its disposal.
3. Push the team to prioritize its key tasks and to allocate assignments among members.
4. Take responsibility for getting important tasks done, and do not wait to be told what to do.
5. On a cross-functional team, ensure that the expertise of all the members is effectively exploited.

Collaborator. At the norming stage, Collaborators wonder whether this era of good feeling is detracting from a focus on the team mission and goals. They agree that positive norms are important and that good feelings and mutual support are necessary. But the real question is "Are we making progress toward our targets?"

The Collaborator sees the establishment of norms as the basis for team members working together for team goals and being willing to share the limelight with each other.

As a Collaborator, you can help the team in a number of ways:

1. Keep the team focused on the big picture.
2. Encourage the team to revisit the mission and goals to determine if the commitment still exists.
3. Be open to altering the mission and revising the goals.
4. Insist that recognition for team efforts be given to all members.
5. Ensure that senior management is aware of the team's progress by providing reports or presentations or both.

Communicator. At this stage, the Communicator feels that the struggle to establish a positive team climate has finally paid off. Shared leadership has emerged, trust is increasing, and conflicts are being resolved. However, there is a concern about "too much of a good thing." The Communicator wonders whether the drive for consensus is masking some real disagreements. He or she senses that members are "walking on eggshells" because they are afraid to damage the effective group process.

If you are a Communicator, here's how you can be useful:

1. Remind the team that disagreements are acceptable and that, in fact, resolving differences is the hallmark of an effective team.
2. Suggest that the team conduct an internal assessment of their team process.
3. Use your feedback skills to point out behaviors that contribute to groupthink.
4. Remind the team that consensus decision making does not require that members simply go along with other members' views.

5. In a teleconference, insist that each person offer his or her opinion on every proposed key decision to ensure a high level of commitment.

Challenger. With groupthink a distinct possibility, the Challenger is alert to the negative norm of reluctance to express differences. As members feel positive about their team and competitive with other teams, the Challenger worries that the tough questions will not be asked. He or she believes that the members can confront each other while still presenting a unified front to the outside world.

As a Challenger, you can help the team at this stage by being willing to take these actions:

1. Ask tough questions, and encourage other members to do the same.
2. Where appropriate, challenge the leader. (This may help establish the norm that challenging is acceptable behavior.) If you are the leader, be open to minority views.
3. Confront the groupthink issue by asking questions that try to uncover real disagreements.
4. Encourage risk taking in team decisions and planning.
5. Be aware that cultural differences may inhibit some people from actively and openly expressing disagreement.

Performing

This is the payoff stage. The team is sailing along; they have learned how to be a team; there is agreement on goals, roles, and norms; and members are aligned toward producing results. The suppression of the storming stage has been worked through, and there is creative confrontation and innovative problem solving.

Moreover, the team is willing periodically to assess its performance and to take corrective action, and members take initiative and responsibility without waiting for direction from the leader.

The team has produced key deliverables on time and achieved other significant milestones. Their progress toward goals is noticeable, so team celebrations take place and recognition comes from other parts of the organization. Ongoing team concerns, however, can include complacency, failure to keep current, and a tendency to slip back into the bad habits of earlier stages. Members often enjoy the road to success or the climb to the summit, but, once they achieve it, look for other worlds to conquer.

Contributor. As the team achieves success, the Contributor sees a tendency to let due dates slip, a failure to complete assignments, and lower attendance at meetings (or the sending of substitutes). He or she also worries that the team will not react quickly or effectively to changes in the external environment. The Contributor wants to be sure the team's skills and resources are sufficient to meet the new challenges.

If you are a Contributor, try to do the following:

1. Push the team to maintain high standards and live up to new task commitments.

2. Suggest that the team examine its resources and consider changing its membership to meet current needs.

3. Suggest that training or other development activities may be needed.

4. Recommend new and challenging task assignments.

Collaborator. Collaborators see the performing stage as a chance to look for opportunities to expand the mission or extend the goals. They correctly see stagnation as a real possibility for the team and, therefore, believe "visioning" new futures may be the answer.

At this stage, the Collaborator can help the team by engaging in some or all of the following:

1. Facilitate brainstorming sessions geared to the creation of a new future for the team.

2. Challenge the team to set aside past restrictions in creating revisions.

3. Ensure that all of the key players participate in this visioning activity.

4. Recommend the development of a new milestone chart.

5. Engage senior management in the development of new or revised purpose for the team.

Communicator. Communicators view the performing stage as the time to celebrate accomplishments. They will play an important role in recommending ways the team can reward itself and in facilitating the involvement of the team members in planning the events. The Communicator, however, is concerned that stagnation indicators (poor attendance, assignments not completed) may lead to "process backsliding" and members' becoming annoyed with each other. For example, a member is mad because her counterpart on the team has been sending a junior person to the meeting in her place. She, in turn, attacks their department at a subsequent meeting. Interpersonal relationships begin to resemble the storming stage.

Useful actions by the Communicator include the following:

1. Encourage positive, uplifting celebrations that involve all team members.

2. Remind the team of the importance of continuing to live by their norms or facilitate the development of a new or revised list of norms.

3. Give positive feedback to members who live up to their commitments.

4. Outside of team meetings, speak to members who show signs of a lack of interest.

Challenger. Challengers are key players at the performing stage because they can address the possible complacency. Although the team success is a source of satisfaction, Challengers worry that the era of good feeling, with its parties and awards, may mask a fear of speaking up. They are also concerned that the team may not react boldly to internal changes (new leader, new members, or new tasks) or to external changes (decreased revenues, increased competition, new regulations) that impact the team.

As a Challenger, you can help if you:

1. Confront the team with indicators of stagnation.
2. Question assumptions of success.
3. Recommend that the team assess its current resources against the work that remains to be done.
4. Initiate a discussion of internal and external changes, their impact on the team, and the implications.

How Team Players Adapt to Team Development

Table 6.1 presents a convenient summary of the relationships between styles and stages. It suggests that each stage of team development evokes different concerns and questions depending on style. Equally important are the series of recommended positive actions for each style at each stage. The effective team player provides the team with the assistance needed in an effort to move the team successfully through the stages toward the goal of performing.

In the next chapter, we combine the concepts of styles and stages in a strategy for analyzing and improving your team.

Table 6.1 How Team Players Adapt to Team Development

Stage	Contributor	Collaborator	Communicator	Challenger
Concerns (F O R M I N G)	My role Expectations of me Time commitments My tasks	Mission of team Goals Leader's vision of team	Membership Acceptance Inclusion Resources of members	Is the team serious? Openness Receptivity to leader
Positive Actions (M I N G)	Initiate discussion of tasks and roles. Ask leader for direction. Offer to take on a start-up assignment.	Ask for leader's views. Offer your view. Suggest a discussion of team mission and goals.	Ask how members were selected. Ask that members introduce themselves. Suggest a team "talent bank."	Ask if team is satisfied with mission. Express your reservations. Suggest a discussion of member concerns.
Concerns (S T O R M I N G)	More heat than light? Will any work get done? Can we be objective?	Can we move forward? Will conflicts lead to failure to help others? Will conflicts dilute commitment?	Will members listen? Will members attack each other? Will members look at both sides?	Will team be receptive to minority opinions? Will leader allow differences to surface? Will team be open to revising its mission?
Positive Actions (M I N G)	Ask for data to support opinions. Remind team of need for homework. Remain objective.	Be willing to help others. Ask how opinions impact team mission. Be open to new ideas.	Model good listening. Suggest norms for resolving conflicts. Encourage the expression of all views.	Model positive confrontational behavior. Be willing to back off when a consensus emerges. Push the team to take well-conceived risks.

(continued)

Table 6.1   (Continued)

Stage	Contributor	Collaborator	Communicator	Challenger
N O R M Concerns	Will standards be maintained? Will all resources be used?	Will the team stay focused on goals? Will we continue to make progress?	Is drive for consensus masking real disagreements? Will emphasis on process go too far?	Will tough questions continue to be asked? Will risk taking be reduced?
M I N G Positive Actions	Insist on high-quality work. Push for priority setting. Take responsibility; don't wait to be asked.	Keep the team focused on the big picture. Ask the team to revisit goals periodically.	Remind the team that consensus does not eliminate disagreement. Suggest an assessment of team process. Use feedback skills.	Ask tough questions and encourage others to do so. Confront groupthink. Encourage risk taking.
P E R F Concerns	Will team slip on responsibilities? Will team react quickly? Will members stay current on issues?	Is it time for a new mission? Does the team need to revise goals?	Will team take the time to acknowledge success? Will members revert to lack of concern for process?	Will team react badly to changes? Will members confront signs of stagnation?
O R M I N G Positive Actions	Push to maintain standards. Propose an examination of needs and resources. Recommend new and challenging assignments.	Facilitate brainstorming sessions focusing on the future.	Initiate positive celebrations of accomplishments. Challenge the team to maintain norms. Give feedback to members.	Confront team with indicators of stagnation. Initiate discussion of environmental changes. Question assumptions of success.

7

ANALYZING YOUR TEAM'S STRENGTHS AND WEAKNESSES

The most effective teams have a balance of team player styles. They are equally concerned with (1) completing their work in a high-quality manner, (2) reaching their goals with a strong commitment, (3) developing and maintaining a positive team climate, and (4) raising questions about the team's goals and methods.

The effective teams know that having balance does not mean equal use of all styles at all times. Balance means having the capability to use the various styles when required by the team. A team's need for a particular style is situational and, as we suggested in Chapter Six, is often based on the stage of team development. Different styles may also be needed at different stages because of new challenges resulting from the reality that

- Team members may not be colocated.
- Teams often include members from a wide variety of functions.
- Members come from different countries and cultures.
- Members often serve on multiple teams.
- Face-to-face meetings are rare, with teleconferencing being the principal meeting format.
- The role of the leader has become both more important and more visible.
- Management expects more from teams than in the past and tends to more closely monitor their progress.

Stages and Styles: The Right Mix at the Right Time

The Collaborator can be especially helpful during the forming stage of a team, when members are concerned about the team's purpose. Members come to the first meeting of a team with questions such as "Why was this team formed?" and "Where are we going?" Teams in the forming stage need someone who can provide structure for a discussion that will culminate in a statement of purpose (charter, mission) and direction (vision, goals, objectives). They also need people who can provide a perspective on management's expectations for the team and potential challenges that exist for a team that is cross-functional and cross-cultural and may have limited opportunities for face-to-face communication and team building.

When conflicts arise in the storming stage, the Communicator can facilitate a resolution of the differences. Team members need to understand that it is OK to express divergent opinions. The most creative teams learn how to resolve conflict in a positive manner—by open discussion of the advantages and disadvantages. Teams in this stage need someone who can both encourage the expression of differences and help the team establish norms for civilized disagreement. They also need someone who can facilitate differences among people with different styles, types of expertise, and cultural norms and who are located in multiple sites linked electronically via email, teleconference, and other similar formal methods.

During the norming stage, the Contributor can help the team establish norms that foster high-quality performance and norms that ensure that members take responsibility for task accomplishment. Following the storming phase, meetings are fun, and competitive cohesion develops as the team feels superior to other teams. At this point, the team needs to focus on getting the job done while they maintain the positive climate. The team needs a team player who can ensure that the norms (1) take into account the team's cultural diversity and (2) establish an atmosphere of trust, open communication, and participative decision making, thereby ensuring the involvement and commitment of all team members.

The performing stage is the goal of team development, so one might easily assume that once it is reached, no help is needed. At this stage, the team has learned how to be a team; norms are in place; and there is agreement on goals, roles, and tasks. Conflicts are successfully resolved, and the team is making great progress. This is the time for a celebration of accomplishments, but it is also a time to be alert to the possibility of stagnation and regression. The Challenger can help. At this stage, we often begin to see signs of declining interest in the form of missed deadlines, the sending of substitutes (usually junior people) to meetings, and loss of the creative spark. The team needs someone to challenge their complacency, to question assumptions, and to suggest that the old fire, associated with the quest for success, has been lost and needs to be rekindled.

The Goal: Style Diversity

Teams that include all four styles will typically outperform those teams that do not. Covering all four areas means that the team is not subject to the vulnerabilities that can be present when one or two styles are absent during an important period.

It would not be surprising to find teams with excessive strength in one or two styles to the exclusion of others. Most people hire and recruit team members for their similarity of strengths. Most people tend to prefer working with people who have a similar style. Many team leaders do not look to broaden the team's perspective by bringing in people who have different styles. Through this oversight, these leaders unknowingly contribute to the ineffectiveness of the team. Although team leaders usually seek team diversity by recruiting people from a wide variety of disciplines or work experiences, a diversity of technical expertise may not accomplish the goal of diverse team player styles.

Style Overload

When a team has many people with the same primary style and excludes other styles, the result is an excess of team strength in one area. Style overload can mean the team excels in several areas but may be weak in others. Depending on the stage of team development, this lack of balance can have a significant impact on team effectiveness.

Contributor Overload. When a team has an excess of people whose primary style is Contributor, a great deal of work gets done and most of that work will be very high quality. The group is likely to make efficient use of its time and resources. Meetings are short, discussions are brief, and reports are limited but relevant. In lieu of meetings, emails are circulated to team members for comment or web-based document editing tools are employed. When possible, electronic mail, teleconferencing, video conferencing, and web conferencing methods are used in place of face-to-face interaction. There is a free sharing of ideas, information, and skills, and members see each other as colleagues linked by technical expertise in the vein of an academic community.

The downside of Contributor overload is that members become intrigued by the intricacies of technical problems and tend to lose sight of the big picture. They enjoy the problem solving so much that they forget to ask "Why?" The team may lose sight of its goal and how the immediate task, issue, or problem relates to the long-term purpose of the team and the organization. Fear of alienating a colleague may block people from asking tough questions about the team's work or from raising ethical issues. And team teleconferences may be so efficient that they lack the spontaneity and fun associated with effective problem solving and decision making.

Collaborator Overload. Teams at the top of organizations tend to be more strategic in their orientation—with the potential for an excess of people with Collaborator as their primary style. This team feels comfortable with strategy discussions and enjoys blue-sky thinking. An annual strategic planning retreat would be a standard event for this team. They produce elaborate plans with detailed charts, and members of the team use references to the future in their presentations and conversations. All current projects are linked to some aspect of the plan. Team members find clever ways to work around the system to obtain resources or to bend the rules if required by the team; the company newspaper carries pictures and stories about team accomplishments; and members of the team are always asking each other questions such as "What do you need?" and "How can I help?"

Although a major concentration on the future is positive, it is sometimes associated with a low concern for the present (for example, short-term objectives, specific problems, project plans, and corporate requirements). Big-picture people often lack a healthy respect for the solution of technical problems, cultural differences, or reports required by government regulatory bodies. Moreover, Collaborator overload can also mean there is little concern for the fact that individual members need rewards and recognition and have language comprehension challenges that may limit their involvement. The preponderance of overly focused strategic team players sometimes forget that members need to participate in the discussions, obtain recognition for their work, get feedback, and, in a variety of other ways, be acknowledged as people by the team. The strong push for commitment by this type of team can also result in member reluctance to criticize anything.

Communicator Overload. Team meetings with an excess of Communicators are usually relaxed and enjoyable. In fact, this asset of the team is often emphasized, as in a recent meeting notice that assured me, "We will definitely have fun." Members are very concerned with how other members feel about issues being discussed. Phrases such as "Are you comfortable with this?" and "Can you live with it?" are common. High-level listening skills are exhibited as members paraphrase, respond nonverbally, and allow others to finish their thoughts. There are regular process checks as someone will ask, "How are we doing?" In face-to-face meetings Communicator overload is usually associated with "flip-chart mania," as the meeting room walls are covered with chart paper. Most decisions are made by consensus, and shared leadership is the norm.

The downside of fun meetings is that task accomplishment may not be sufficient to satisfy the team's key stakeholders—or some members. Senior management's high expectations may not be satisfied by a team assessment that emphasizes positive feelings over positive work output. Some team members may even wonder whether there should not be more output for the time spent by the team and may be further concerned that member contributions could be limited by the fact that so many people are simultaneously serving on several other teams. They may even wonder if there is not a way to get some work done while having fun! The context may be missing; the process is good, but to what end? These teams may forget that a positive climate is means to an end and not the goal of a team.

Challenger Overload. When a team has an excess of people with Challenger as their primary style, rank does not have any privileges. Members are outspoken and even critical of the team leader. There are no controversies "swept under the rug" and no hidden agendas. Candor and openness are the norm. These teams tend to be very creative, even innovative in a variety of ways, and they support and encourage risk taking; failures are not punished. Assessments of team progress are honest and carefully scrutinized by team members. Team meetings are marked by pointed questions about goals, plans, and process. Members from all countries are encouraged to provide input on how their market and culture will impact the product or service being developed by the team.

However, Challenger overload can also result in candor for the sake of candor. The team can get bogged down in always focusing on what is wrong. Members may look for problems rather than strengths or opportunities (the glass is always half empty rather than half full). The outside world can eventually see them as a group of whiners or weirdos who always seem to be against everything.

Missing Perspectives

Another tool for analyzing your team is to look for the missing perspective—the one style that does not exist with any degree of strength. The absence of the strengths incorporated in that style will result in an imbalance leading to decreased effectiveness, missed opportunities, poor use of team resources, and even dissatisfaction among team members. The missing perspective is especially significant during the stage of team development when that style is most needed.

Contributor Is Missing. The main problem likely to emerge on a team with no Contributor is the lack of task focus. The team will not be serious about getting the necessary work done in an efficient manner; there will be a poor use of time and resources, meetings will not be well planned and organized, and ultimately there will be a ripple effect—the few people who do complete their assignments will become resentful of those who do not, and eventually even the effective few will lower their standards. And during the start-up of a new team or the re-forming of an existing team, members will fail to establish clarity on role definition and expectations. Members who are also on several other teams will give the work of this team a lower priority, further decreasing team productivity. Trust among members will suffer.

Collaborator Is Missing. Especially at the outset of the formation of a team with no Collaborator, there will be a lack of clarity about perspective and purpose. When the Collaborator style is missing, a new team is likely to flounder and lose interest because goals are not formulated. In general, the team is characterized by nonexistent or unclear mission and goals. Members have a go-it-alone mentality; there is no crossover assistance from people in other functional areas. Lack of the collaborative perspective also means that only the team leader or a few of the members get the recognition for team accomplishments. Again, trust will be adversely affected. In the end, other team members become resentful because of the uneven distribution of credit for the team's success. Senior management, with high expectations for the team, will lose interest in the project and begin to shift resources to other teams.

Communicator Is Missing. If there is no Communicator, the team climate is formal, even tense, with a corresponding low level of interpersonal comfort. Interactions among members are task- and goal-based, with little concern for process issues. There is plenty of talking and presenting of ideas but not much listening or responding to each other. Few decisions are made by the consensus method; most issues are decided by a small minority or by major- ity vote. Genuine participation by members is neither emphasized nor encouraged by the leader or members; as a result, involvement is limited. Lack of participation is especially prominent among people whose language differences make it difficult to under- stand some of the discussions. Team success is measured by task completion. There is little positive recognition or praise for indi- vidual contribution or team accomplishments, and the prevailing philosophy is "It's your job and that's what we pay you for."

Challenger Is Missing. With no one around to challenge the conventional wisdom, the tendency for groupthink (Janus, 1972) is great because the team culture includes strong pressures to conform. Similarly, "The Abilene Paradox" described by Jerry Harvey (1974, p. 23) in his classic article holds that teams often do things "in contradiction to the data they have for dealing with problems and, as a result, compound their problems." Team mem- bers do not express their reservations, because they believe they are the only ones who feel that way. It is paradoxical because there is no conformity pressure. The need for the Challenger's strengths is especially apparent in the performing stage, when the team has achieved some success and the members are feeling good about their progress. With senior management now having a much higher level of expectations for teams than in the past, the team may wink at ethical constraints, questionable data, or legal obstacles in the surge to complete their work by the deadline but there is also a tendency to play it safe in an effort to ensure their success. Risk taking may not be encouraged and surely will not be rewarded, so there's a great likelihood of unimaginative solutions and team stagnation. Unless challenged to reexamine their goals and methods, the team may retreat, members will lose interest, and some may drop out or give priority to other assignments.

How to Analyze Your Team

The team leader, in concert with the members, may analyze the team using the concept of team player styles. The team looks for the potential for style overload and the possibility of a missing style; once the team has identified the situation, they can assess the implications. For example, if your team is overloaded with Contributors, how has this affected team decision making, planning, problem solving, communicating, and risk taking? On the other hand, if the team does not include the Contributor perspective, how has this adversely affected the operation of the team? When possible, try to use actual examples from the team's recent history to assess the impact.

Table 7.1 includes two sample team profiles. All team members have completed the *Parker Team Player Survey*, and the location of the "X" indicates their primary team player styles.

In Sample Team Profile I, five of the eight team members are Contributors, and there are no Challengers on the team.

- What are the implications of their profile in terms of strengths and weaknesses?
- What do you suspect the team will do well?
- Where are the team's "blind spots" and potential weaknesses?

Table 7.1 Analyzing a Team Profile

Sample Team Profile I: Contributor Overload/Challenger Is Missing

Name/Style	Contributor	Collaborator	Communicator	Challenger
Glen			X	
Dick		X		
Ira	X			
Peg	X			
Sylvie	X			
Maria	X			
Terry			X	
Judy	X			

Exercise: 1. *Analysis.* Identify the strengths and weaknesses of this team in terms of the following:
   a. Planning
   b. Communication
   c. Risk taking
   d. Problem solving
   e. Decision making
2. *Action Planning.* Recommend possible improvements for this team.

Sample Team Profile II: Collaborator Overload/Communicator Is Missing

Name/Style	Contributor	Collaborator	Communicator	Challenger
Jill		X		
Ellen	X			
Michael		X		
Eduardo		X		
Roberto		X		
Wilhelm				X
David		X		
Kim	X			

Exercise: 1. *Analysis.* Identify the strengths and weaknesses of the team in terms of the following:
   a. Planning
   b. Communication
   c. Risk taking
   d. Problem solving
   e. Decision making
2. *Action Planning.* Recommend possible improvements for this team.

- If you know of such a team, can you cite some team actions that reflect either the overload of task orientation or the absence of anyone willing to raise questions about the team?

In Sample Team Profile II, five of the eight team members are Collaborators, and there are no Communicators.

- What are the implications of this mix for the success of the team?
- What do you think the team will do well?
- Where are the team's "blind spots" and potential weaknesses?
- Think of some teams that you believe may have this style composition. What do they do well? In what areas are they weak?

8

DEVELOPING A TEAM PLAYER CULTURE

> I strongly believe that people will exhibit behaviors
> that get recognized and rewarded.
>> —*Human resources manager, Johnson & Johnson,*
>> *survey response*

Many people in our original survey population believe that team rewards and individual member recognition are the best ways to encourage effective team play. But differences arise in identifying the best method, and there is a gap between the approaches currently used by companies and those that are believed to work best. In our survey of major corporations, we asked people to indicate methods they currently use to create a team player culture. We also asked for a list of recommended methods—approaches they have not yet tried but ones they believe will work. See Table 8.1 for a comparison.

Current Methods

In this section we provide a description of current methods used to create and sustain a team-oriented culture in an organization, followed by some methods recommended by survey respondents and others that are designed to address the new realities and challenges of teamwork as described earlier in this book.

Table 8.1 Current and Recommended Methods of Developing a Team Player Culture

Current	*Recommended*
1. Public Statement by Top Management	1. Promotion
2. Important Assignments	2. Upper Management as Team Player Models
3. Training and Development	3. Performance Appraisal
4. Promotion	4. Rewards and Recognition

Public Statements by Top Management. Teamwork is highly valued in organizations. Speeches at corporate meetings are filled with references to success being the result of "all of us pulling together." Upper-level management refers to the company "family" and the efforts of "all members of the team" in reaching the organization's goals. Many people have sent me copies of company newspapers and annual reports that contain statements by corporate leaders acknowledging the importance of effective team players. It is important that public messages promote the value of team players and that, at award ceremonies, such messages address the specific contributions of individuals who are outstanding team players. The organization needs to hear from its leaders about the type of performance that is rewarded. As one of our survey respondents said, "We make it clear that good team play is expected and is necessary to meet our objectives."

Important Assignments. Because we know that team players like responsibility and a challenge and to be part of something important, one current method of encouragement is to give top team players important assignments, such as leading a new "heavyweight" (that is, high-priority) team. Some people see this as the best approach because it is a means to producing better team players. If we can believe all of the so-called motivation-to-work survey results, then rewarding team players with better work opportunities makes great sense. One work-motivation study reported "opportunity to produce quality work (93%)" and "feeling that my work is important (89%)" at the top of a rank-order list of motivators (*Metrex Footnotes*, 1988, p. 3).

Training and Development. Many companies provide workshops in communication skills, meetings management, listening, assertiveness, conflict resolution, goal setting, and other topics that provide the skills necessary to be an effective team player. Some organizations also offer team-building consulting services to project teams and other important business teams. Although these development opportunities send a message that the organization supports teamwork, it is not a strong message unless it is coupled with other corporate activities. In some companies, unfortunately, cynics often see team workshops as "that touchy-feely stuff" produced by human resources.

Few sessions focus specifically on being a team player. Current workshops primarily address the effective team, the effective leader, or communication/leadership skills. More sessions are needed on the role of team player, increasing team player effectiveness, and the dimensions of an effective team. It is not surprising that this kind of training was not selected by any of our survey respondents as a recommended motivator of team players. Clearly, although many companies offer workshops in this area, training by itself is not perceived to be an effective incentive for the encouragement of teamwork and team play.

Recommended Strategies

Some years ago, a colleague, David Jamieson, developed an approach to creating and sustaining a team-based organization that brings together a number of important elements (Jamieson, 1996). The Jamieson model includes four elements: (1) strategy, (2) structure, (3) systems, and (4) culture.

Strategy

Strategy—the organization's approach to reaching its objectives—must include teamwork and team players as integral building blocks. A teamwork strategy says that the organization believes that effective teams are important factors in our ability to develop new products, compete in the global marketplace, provide quality customer service, and, in the end, enhance sales and profitability.

Beyond the articulation of a team-based strategy is the adoption of this strategy by everyone in the organization, but most important, by the senior management team. The senior leadership team, in turn, holds their managers accountable for the implementation of the strategy. Accountability leads to the appropriate and necessary behaviors being exhibited by everyone in the organization.

In one of my most challenging assignments, a senior-level manager in a telecommunications company said he thought the company's vision statement, which emphasized the value of teamwork, was in need of a good dose of reality. He had been part of a series of meetings that produced the vision document, and he was afraid that it was in danger of becoming just one more corporate manifesto, doomed to gather dusk on office bookshelves. He proposed a project (later named "turning vision into reality") that would embed teamwork and team players in the organization such that it became simply "the way we do business." The challenge for organizations is to:

1. Say the right words and mean it ("talk the talk").
2. Act as if you mean it ("walk the talk").

Talk the Talk. Organizations that believe in teamwork must continually send a clear and consistent message that we support teamwork and we value team players. Leaders and managers should use every opportunity to communicate this message—including corporate "town hall" meetings, video conference company updates, and manager training meetings, as well as regular staff meetings. It is important for managers to breathe life into elements of the strategy statement that focus on teamwork, as in the following excerpts from three corporate strategy or vision documents:

> Quality is our priority and teamwork is our standard in all aspects of what we do.

> Our goal is to establish a climate of openness, mutual respect and teamwork.

> We seek teamwork throughout the organization . . . participative goal-setting . . . decision-making at the lowest level.

In addition, company publications should be used to communicate the strategy in terms of daily corporate life. Stories about effective teams and outstanding team players should appear in the company newspaper, business unit newsletter, annual report, corporate magazine, and closed-circuit television station. Repetition is important because employees can become cynical about management fads, often referred to as the "program *du jour*" or "flavor of the month." Employees have seen new programs and new managers come and go and their reaction can be "if I just wait for a while, a new 'thing' will come down the road." Therefore, every opportunity to "talk the talk" should be used to underscore the importance and sustainability of teamwork and team players.

Walk the Talk. Cynics will say "talk is cheap." And I agree, but it is the place to start. However, it cannot end there. The leadership team must live by the words. First, they must act and work like a team. They must be a model of effective teamwork, and each member of the team must be a positive team player. They must set the standard and be the beacon of light that all in the organization can see as the way everyone is expected to act. We know that the behavior of your manager is a very important motivator of employee behavior. If your manager is ethical, you are likely to be ethical; if your manager is customer-focused, you are likely to be customer-focused; similarly, if your manager is a team player, then you are more likely to also be a team player.

Some years ago, on my first visit to the corporate headquarters of a major global company, I noticed that every office and conference room displayed a framed copy of the company values. I mentioned to my client that this was quite impressive, to which he replied, "And the CEO monitors every decision to ensure it is consistent with those values." Later I wondered how he, as a mid-level manager, knew anything about how the CEO operated. The point was that he probably did not know it from direct experience, but he believed it! And you can be sure my client checked every one of his decisions to ensure consistency with those values.

By contrast, at another organization I was facilitating a team building session where we talked about working more effectively with their colleagues across functional lines. The people at the session, all middle managers, responded with "You better tell our bosses first." They went on to tell horror stories of directions from their supervisors to not work with this group, to hold up work needed by another, or to withhold information from another. The message was clear in this organization: we talk the teamwork talk but we don't walk the talk.

Structure

Structure is the way we organize people and work to implement the strategy. It is the shape of the organization, including the relationships among work, people, and technology. In a pure team-based organization, teams replace departments and functions. For example, the organization no longer has a customer service function but rather is composed of teams responsible for a region, market, customer, or line of business. There are few true team-based organizations. Most organizations operate with a structure that includes functional departments that provide either easy access or significant barriers to cross-organizational collaboration. The key element in structure is the ease with which communication and collaboration across functional lines can be facilitated. The manager's behavior is critical here. The manager can support teamwork and team players by

- Communicating with clarity to associates in his or her area that being an effective player on cross-functional teams is valued and will be rewarded
- Empowering associates to make decisions and commit resources on behalf of the function
- Facilitating the participation of associates on teams by adjusting their work priorities and time schedules so they can be effective team players on cross-functional teams
- Actively soliciting feedback about the performance of associates on cross-functional teams and incorporating that information in their performance review
- Recognizing associates who are effective team players on cross-functional teams
- Demonstrating interest in the work of their associates on teams in a number of ways, including such things as periodically meeting with associates to discuss the work of their teams

Many companies in our survey reported that the top leadership in their organizations talked about the importance of team players to the success of the enterprise. Although statements about the need for teamwork are necessary, they alone are not sufficient. Our survey participants, including both top executives and mid-level managers, felt that "actions speak louder than words." And though that phrase may not mark a dramatic conceptual breakthrough, everyone agrees that, in organizations, people watch closely the behaviors of their leaders. In other words, they both "read their lips" and watch their actions.

As a consultant, I have heard many managers complain about the lack of cooperation among the executive team members. For example, a manager will see or hear about the executives' failure to work together. Occasionally, a manager will get an informal directive from his or her vice president not to give information or in other ways to not help people in other functional organizations. In such cases, top management is not acting cooperatively and is discouraging its staff from practicing positive team play. Very quickly, people in the organization get the message—"We may talk about the value of teamwork, but we don't practice it." Clearly, however, positive modeling does work. When the leadership works as a team, being a team player becomes the organizational norm. Modeling is especially important in today's world where cross-functional, global teams abound, making collaboration across functional areas at the management level essential to effective teamwork.

Another survey respondent strongly emphasized the need for top management's "actually emulating 'teamplayership' with their staff *and* encouraging them to assist others beyond their normal responsibility." And the former president of a major food company said, "It requires a strong message, in words and actions, from senior management."

Systems

All systems in the organization must be aligned and in support of teamwork. You cannot have a strategy that emphasizes teamwork and team players and a structure that encourages cross-organizational collaboration that is not supported by the relevant organizational systems. Relevant systems consist of information and performance management, including promotions, training, and rewards.

Information. An information system in which information flows primarily one way—up—must be rerouted. Teams cannot be held accountable for certain work products if they cannot get accurate and timely information. Information must flow up, down, and laterally to teams so they can complete their work and measure the results. People in the organization must be held accountable for information-sharing; it must be incorporated in the performance appraisal systems.

Performance Management. It is important to include team player behaviors in the corporate performance appraisal form. In addition, a person's performance on a team must be incorporated in the person's overall appraisal. The functional manager responsible for the appraisal must get feedback from team leaders on the performance of team members from that functional department. Initially, the organization may, as one of our clients did, implement a team performance management process whereby the project team leader completes a form for each team member that assesses that member's performance on the team against a series of specific team player behaviors. The leader meets with each member and then provides the form to the functional area manager. In this model, team members also rate the performance of the team leader which, in turn, is provided to the manager of team leaders.

When the organization reaches the high performing stage, some form of peer appraisal may be added to the process (McGee, 1998). In peer appraisal, team members provide performance feedback about their teammates. The information on the peer feedback forms is incorporated in the associate's overall performance management process. For example, at the milk plant of H-E-B Grocery, Bob McCullough, vice president of manufacturing, reports that "our process for our team members is a 360 process so the team members evaluate each other. They are part of the annual performance evaluation for each other. Who [better] knows how

well each team member is working than his or her teammates?"
(Dudlicek, 2003, p. 30).

Performance management is very important because it is a
well-established corporate activity that tells employees how their
performance is valued. As a result, it is critical that specific team
player behaviors be included among the factors that are rated.
Many companies are already including team behaviors in their
appraisal forms. Here are some example behaviors:

- Understands and supports the goals of the team
- Consults with others and shares information
- Negotiates differences effectively
- Constructively challenges prevailing points of view
- Is open to unsolicited points of view
- Is friendly and approachable in working with others

There is widespread agreement that those behaviors valued by the organization must be included in the performance
appraisal process. Although words like *teamwork* and *cooperation*
are included in some appraisal forms, the meaning of these terms
is not clear. If *team player* is incorporated as a performance factor,
then the behaviors to be assessed should be specified. The list of
behaviors outlined in Chapter Three would be a place to start.
Several companies in our survey provided us with their appraisal
forms, and those forms defined behaviors aligned with our view of
team players. One company assesses the following factors:

- *Flexibility*. Responsive to unscheduled requests. Able to shift
  tasks and maintain priorities. Adjusts to changing situations
  without undue stress or complaint.
- *Innovativeness*. Creatively develops new approaches to
  problems. Recommends efficiencies and new systems. Perceives
  and creates opportunities for improving job performance.

- *Risk Taking*. Decisive and willing to proceed without all available data. Appropriately operates outside of existing procedures.
- *Teamwork*. Effective as a team member. Constructively challenges prevailing points of view. Solicits supporting expertise as necessary.
- *Initiative and Drive*. Self-starter. Seeks out opportunities to influence events. High energy level.

Although this company has *teamwork* as one of the performance factors, behaviors in all other categories are also associated with team players—most notably, the *risk-taking* actions we would associate with the Challenger, *flexibility* associated with the Collaborator, and *innovativeness* associated with the Contributor role. However, this form does not include the process behavior contributed by the Communicator.

Another company does include the team-process behaviors of the Communicator in its appraisal form. The following are some of the team player factors incorporated in their appraisal system:

- *Relationships*. Builds trust. Is friendly and approachable in working with others in and outside of work group.
- *Innovation*. Solves problems creatively. Seeks, develops, and encourages new ideas.
- *Participation*. Actively seeks the best solution by asking for ideas. Is open to unsolicited ideas and opinions. Offers ideas. Contributes actively as a team member. Inspires teamwork in others.
- *Accountability*. Holds self responsible for understanding and meeting expectations. Takes initiative to identify and solve problems without blaming others.
- *Spirit*. Is enthusiastic about work. Excites others through example.

These few examples demonstrate that it is possible to use the performance appraisal process as a strategy for encouraging people to be team players and thereby to establish teamwork as a corporate norm. More still can be done in this vein to support and develop team players. For example, it is now important to be able to communicate with people from different countries and cultures, juggle priorities emanating from membership on multiple teams, build trust quickly with teammates around the world, and effectively connect with people via email, teleconferences, and other remote methods.

Related to the appraisal process should be development planning. In many companies, each person has a development plan that indicates targeted future positions and activities designed to enhance the person's career development opportunities. Here is another area in which team player behavior can be reinforced. The development plan can emphasize the need for team player behaviors and can include training, projects, and assignments designed to improve the needed skills and knowledge. In addition, the training workshops sponsored by the human resources department can be a useful supplement and support for the more powerful organizational development interventions.

Promotions. Many companies report that they promote people who are team players and are technically competent. This method overlaps the two categories—promotions are currently being used as a reward, and they are recommended as a way of further motivating people to be more effective team players.

In our survey, a vice president of human resources says it directly: "We promote team players . . . [and] we make it clear that profit-goal accomplishment alone will not lead to promotion."

A promotion is a specific, visible reward, and it can be used both to reward team players and to send a message to others in the organization that team player behaviors are valued. However, promotion by itself is not enough. The reasons for the promotion must be made clear and specific. When a person is promoted because he or she is both technically competent and an effective team player, the accomplishments in both areas should be highlighted. Here is an example of a short announcement that has been edited to protect the anonymity of the people involved:

Donna Jamieson
Promoted to Project Director

Donna Jamieson has been promoted to project manager in recognition of her creativity as a systems developer on PBAT, YAM, and ORRIS. She continues to develop her technical skills via in-company workshops and external seminars, and she recently completed course requirements for an M.S. degree in computer science from S.U. As cochair of the user interface team and a member of the BIRKS Task Force, Donna has shown herself to be someone who can be depended on to do her homework, to pitch in when other people need help, and to make sure everyone gets a chance to participate in team decisions. She is honest, ethical, sensitive to cultural diversity issues on teams, and willing to speak her mind on important organizational issues. Donna contributes technical excellence as well as a positive team spirit to our organization.

It is important that everyone know that being an effective team player contributed to Donna's promotion. The promotion and the text of the announcement make it clear that team players are valued and that getting ahead in this organization requires a demonstrated competence in both technical and team player skills.

One of the respondents to our survey went to the other end of the spectrum. He recommended the "removal from positions of authority managers who are not team players." Similarly, when this type of action is contemplated, the positioning and the associated message must indicate that poor teamwork caused the removal.

Training and Development. Training sends a message of organizational commitment. Providing opportunities for team training for leaders and members, as well as team building for intact teams, tells people that teamwork is so important that we are prepared to invest in their development in this area. Learning opportunities must also include programs for senior management that provide advice on how to support teams and team players in their organization. For example, in one pharmaceutical company we conducted three programs: (1) a team leader workshop, (2) a team member workshop, and (3) a seminar for the senior leadership team. In each of the three programs, the participants learned about effective teamwork from the perspective of their role. For example, team leaders learned how to facilitate a team meeting, team members learned how to be effective meeting participants, and the leadership team learned what they could do to support teamwork and team players in the organization. The concepts were the same, but the focus differed.

A recent study of training for virtual teams produced some interesting results (Beranek and Martz, 2005). The training consisted of three parts:

1. Teamwork meetings and collaboration technologies in the context of the model of Drexler and others (1998)
2. The disadvantages of electronic communications such as leaner communication channels (such as lack of nonverbal cues)
3. Examples of common "ebbreviations" to assist in electronic communication (such as use of "emoticons" to denote humor)

The authors concluded, after measuring team members' attitudes over four time periods, that the training helped ". . . improve group cohesiveness, perceptions of group process and satisfaction with the team's outcomes" (Beranek and Martz, 2005, p. 207).

Rewards and Recognition. We make a distinction between rewards and recognition for teams and team players (Parker, McAdams, and Zielinski, 2003). Rewards are acknowledgment of successful team performance *based on a pre-announced formula.* In the vernacular, we say rewards are based on the concept of "do this and get that." If the team accomplishes an objective (for example, delivering a new software package on time and bug-free), every member of the team receives a reward (such as a gift of a specified value from a catalogue). You can also take this rewards concept company-wide, as in the case of Providian Financial, a San Francisco–based financial services company. If the company decreases customer turnover by 50 percent in one year, *every employee* receives a $500 bonus (Kador, 2001). The goal of the company is to encourage cross-functional collaboration among employees.

Recognition, on the other hand, is an *after-the-fact* acknowledgment of outstanding performance by an entire team or an individual team player. In colloquial speech, we might say, "I caught you doing something right." Both types of acknowledgment have their place, and both have their critics. And you can combine rewards and recognition. For example, some companies have a rewards program for project teams at the same time that they may recognize individual team players who did some extraordinary work for the team or who, although not team members, provided the team with work that was critical to overall success of the project team.

Team recognition through awards is a controversial suggestion. Some companies include team awards in the corporate awards program. They firmly believe such awards promote teamwork by recognizing the efforts of specific work groups or task forces. These awards usually involve cash payments plus other items such as plaques, team pictures, and stories in the company newspapers.

Opponents argue that award programs are divisive. They believe that people who do not get awards can become angry and unproductive and that the net result is discouragement. In the opponents' view only "hot" projects are recognized, and many people are on teams that are just "toiling in the vineyards"— performing the basic work of the company—and have no chance for an award. The opponents of team awards see politics influencing the decisions and believe that upper management cannot clearly see the good work done by teams (Kohn, 1993).

I believe it is not helpful to create a dichotomy whereby an organization is forced to choose between team rewards and no team rewards. Rather, I support the conclusion of a study of five Motorola sites around the world (Scottsdale, Arizona; Schaumberg, Illinois; Fort Worth, Texas; Dublin, Ireland; and Hong Kong): "[T]eam rewards were a necessary but insufficient ingredient of team success. In fact, employee involvement and empowerment were identified as the most vital ingredients of real team effectiveness" (Gedvilas, 1997, p. 6).

The organization needs to start with an agreement that people exhibit the behaviors that are rewarded and recognized. In addition, the organization's formal awards program should allow teams to win awards and encourage them to enter; it should also revise the criteria for individual recognition to include team player behaviors.

One of the keys to a successful rewards and recognition program is allowing team members to select their own rewards as long as they stay within a budgetary limit. There are many catalogues that companies can use to implement an effective rewards and recognition program. An alternative to the catalogue that also gives employees a choice is a general gift certificate from one of the credit-card companies. Although some people believe that only money is valued as a reward, studies continually show that employees want recognition for their contributions to the company. Noncash rewards provide recognition from management and peers. And perhaps more important, the recognition factor ("trophy value") lasts long after the money has been spent. In one company, where the program provides cash awards, people also receive a plaque, which serves as a permanent reminder of the recognition.

In the Motorola study just cited, the types of team recognition identified as helpful included ". . . thank yous, team and group celebrations, individual spot bonuses and individual and group presentations of non-cash awards, such as trips, dinners and coffee mugs" (Gedvilas, 1997, p. 8).

There are many nonmonetary forms of reward that encourage and support team player behaviors. (By the way, this discussion assumes that people in the organization perceive the fundamental financial rewards to be adequate and fair. No form of recognition will work unless these basic needs are being addressed.)

Technical and scientific personnel are often the least interested in teamwork. They enjoy working alone and are rewarded for their individual achievements. Yet, as Mower and Wilemon (1989) have shown, technical professionals will work together when there is thoughtful recognition for their efforts and especially when there is respect from their peers. Some examples of these types of recognition include publicity in newspapers and company publications, a commendation presented at a company meeting and a plaque or certificate that cites the person's or team's achievements.

These forms of recognition tend to appeal to extrinsic motivation; they are external rewards. However, extrinsic rewards (1) can be overused to the point where they lose value, (2) are seen by some recipients as manipulative, and (3) are just not effective with people who are turned off by external recognition. Many technical professionals and others are more motivated by internal rewards such as challenging work, increased responsibility, and an opportunity to learn. For organizations that wish to appeal to team players' intrinsic motivation, Mower and Wilemon (1989) suggest such things as asking a person or team to take on a difficult assignment, increasing the scope of a team's mission, or seeking the team's advice on a major challenge or opportunity.

Team recognition works as a supporter of team player behaviors only when the mission of the team requires real task interdependence. In other words, the work can be completed satisfactorily only if members share expertise, set joint goals, regularly interact, and are willing to raise questions and challenge each other. Some teams are really not teams but simply groups of people tied together by what we have referred to as administrative convenience. These groups are teams in name only because the work is a series of discrete tasks that do not require any coordination.

When real teamwork is required, recognition can be a powerful motivator for effective team players. And most important from an organizational standpoint, "Teams rewarded on a strictly team basis, with everybody sharing equally, almost always outperform teams in which certain persons are rewarded more than others" (Mower and Wilemon, 1989, pp. 27–28).

One final but important factor in team rewards and recognition is the selection process. I recommend a peer review process that is controlled by nonmanagement employees, such as the Peer Recognition Awards Program devised some years ago by General Electric's Space Systems Division in Philadelphia and replicated by other companies. An employee peer review board develops the award guidelines, reviews all proposals, makes the decisions, and announces the awards. One company also includes a few management people on the committee to ensure an organizational perspective and alignment of the awards with corporate objectives. This company also rotates committee membership so that all employees learn how the program works in practice.

Salary Increases. Tangible rewards do not have to come in the form of an award or cash bonus. Salary treatment is another approach. If the appraisal system and development planning use the team player behaviors in their decision making, it makes sense to give higher merit increases and salary adjustments to employees who perform well in both job task accomplishment and team player skills. Again, the employee should be told the reason for the salary decision as a way of reinforcing the appropriate behaviors.

Compensation Systems. As discussed in Chapter One, even selling—that most individualistic of occupations—is moving to a team approach. With many salespeople working on a single account, compensation must support and encourage teamwork and ensure fair treatment for each person. Cespedes, Doyle, and Freedman (1989), who studied four companies with sizable sales forces, argue for flexibility in compensation systems, with different approaches for different types of accounts. For example, "If there are many salespeople calling on key accounts and teamwork is important, then a bonus based on total account sales often makes more sense than traditional, individually oriented incentive arrangements" (p. 46). Another problem is with large accounts. Teamwork is usually required, and closing the sales can take months, even years. And because most compensation systems are geared to short-term results, salespeople are not encouraged to work as a team on these large accounts. However, Cespedes, Doyle, and Freedman point out that "bonuses for multi-year performance, or for qualitative objectives like building relationships with certain account decision-makers, can encourage team effort" (p. 46).

Management Assessment Program. Some companies include teamwork as a competency factor in their assessment center programs. Anheuser-Busch, for example, incorporates team-related competencies (for example, group management) as part of its management competency model. If the assessment program is aimed at identifying people for leadership positions in the company, then team player skills should be measured along with such competencies as problem solving, creativity, and communication.

Eliminate Competitive Rating Systems. Rating and ranking systems that pit employees against each other in the annual performance review process tend to work against the development of teamwork. A ranking system that includes a requirement for a bell-shaped-curve distribution further emphasizes competition over cooperation.

Under this system, employees know that in the final analysis, their performance will be compared with that of other employees—even those on the same work team. This fact alone affects their willingness to be effective team players. Many employees have told me that they are reluctant to share technical expertise because it may help another person obtain a better rating and a higher rank. Many employees ask, "Why should I be a team player when my appraisal is based solely on my individual contribution?"

Two employees who had to work together throughout the year and enjoyed being team players tried an experiment. During the year, all of their work (reports, programs, and memos) was published under joint authorship. They accomplished a great deal and were satisfied with their effort as a team. However, in preparation for the annual division appraisal meeting, their manager asked that they indicate specifically who prepared each document. The system required that there be some way of differentiating them!

Culture

Culture has been defined as "the way we do things around here" (Deal and Kennedy, 1982). It includes and is influenced by a web of elements such as the business environment, values, stories, myths, heroes, heroines, norms, and a network of "carriers." A strong culture tells people in the organization how to behave in most situations; it tells team players

- What the organization values
- Who the organization values
- How they are supposed to behave
- Who the "stars" of the organization are
- How success is defined
- Who will get rewarded
- What will get rewarded

If your organization has long valued individual technical excellence, thinly veiled competition, solo action, and private agreements, then there is a need to emphasize sharing information, working collaboratively, making decisions in a participative manner, and valuing empowerment. A body of teamwork stories will then evolve and circulate; the stories will recognize as heroes and heroines those team players who helped the crowd stand out rather than those whose goal is to stand out themselves.

There is a crucial link between culture and strategy. An organization's culture must be aligned with the strategy if the strategy is to have any chance of succeeding. If you have a team-based strategy, the values and, specifically, the norms of the organization must emphasize collaboration, consensus, and communication. There is a crucial link between culture and structure. If the structure facilitates free and easy collaboration across organizational lines, then the culture must make heroes and heroines of team leaders who succeed at managing a diverse group of people from a variety of functions. There is also a crucial link between culture and systems; for example:

- If the culture values information sharing, then teams will get the information they need to complete their tasks and achieve their objectives.
- If the culture values people who are team players, then the performance appraisal process will incorporate those behaviors into the system.
- If the culture values global teamwork, then the rewards and recognition program will acknowledge team leaders and members who can work with people from a diverse group of countries, who have the technical and interpersonal skills to make effective use of new communications technologies, and who can develop trusting and effective relationships with representatives from many different functions and disciplines.

R$_x$ for the Development of a Team Player Culture

1. Having corporate leaders make public statements on the importance of team players and teamwork to business success
2. Asking executives and senior managers to serve as role models of positive team players

3. Promoting people who are both technically competent and team players, with appropriate public announcements that emphasize team player skills as an important factor in the promotions

4. Giving important assignments to positive team players

5. Incorporating team player behaviors in the performance appraisal system

6. Providing training workshops on the skills of an effective team player, leading a global virtual team, and building trust quickly among people from different cultures

7. Giving higher salary increases to positive team players

8. Developing incentive systems that reward team results and effective collaboration by individual team members

9. Designing flexible compensation programs that pay individuals for their contributions to a team approach

10. Including team player competencies in the management assessment process

11. Developing a program of team awards that are tailored to the motivational needs of the organization

12. Encouraging managers to use a variety of nonmonetary forms of recognition that appeal to intrinsic motivation

13. Eliminating competitive rating and ranking performance appraisal systems that do not value team player contributions

9

CHALLENGES FOR TEAMS AND TEAM PLAYERS

Teamwork does not happen by accident. People are not born to be team players. As Alfie Kohn (1986) has shown, many people—most particularly Americans—are trained to be competitive rather than cooperative. Organizations that adopt teamwork as a strategy for success must develop plans for meeting the challenges at various levels of the organization.

The Executive Challenge

Leaders at the top of the house must be prepared to say the right words and then make them come alive on a daily basis. Many organizations adopt a vision statement or a list of corporate values. These statements usually call for teamwork, quality, customer service, and other admirable goals. Copies of the statements are found in company publications and are usually displayed in prominent company locations. *Such statements are necessary but not sufficient.* Executives who want team play to be a way of life must examine every important decision in light of its impact on that concept.

Visitors at the corporate offices of a major pharmaceutical company in New Jersey find a framed copy of the Corporate Values on the wall of every office and conference room. The statement says that the company values include teamwork throughout the organization; participative goal setting, measurement, feedback; and decision making at the lowest level. Visitors are also told that the CEO measures each executive decision for its consistency with both the spirit and content of the values. All executives and managers throughout the organization are expected to do the same.

However, the world has changed since I first experienced this company and its emphasis on "living the values." Today, as Bill George, former CEO of Medtronic, says in his new book (George and Sims, 2007), it is not about "me" (executive) but about "we" (team). The challenge for executives is not to get people to follow them but to empower others (such as team leaders) to lead. The new, more effective style is collaboration and participation rather than command and control. However, although the emphasis now is on a team-based approach, that strategy has led to a culture of rising expectations for teams. The new culture, combined with major changes in the business landscape, has made team success more difficult. As we have said throughout the book, these changes include the following:

- The number and variety of cross-functional teams has increased dramatically.
- An increasing number of teams are global in nature and therefore have a multicultural membership.
- Virtual teams are much more common.
- Teams are more dependent on communications technology, such as email, teleconferencing, video conferencing, and web conferencing.
- Team trust is now both more difficult to achieve and more critical to team success.
- Team meetings are more important and more challenging due to the cross-functional, cross-cultural, and virtual nature of teams.
- Teams require a supportive organizational environment that includes a team-based strategy, structure, systems, and culture.

- Team players serve on multiple cross-functional teams in addition to their functional work team.
- As a result of all of these changes, team leadership is both more difficult and more important.

The Management Challenge

Managers must act in ways that support team players. When task forces, committees, and business teams are formed, managers should look for diversity of team player styles in selecting team members and for a leader with solid technical expertise combined with high-level interpersonal skills. Managers should insist on a support system for teams that includes the following factors:

- Performance on teams is included in each person's overall performance appraisal.
- Team player behaviors are incorporated in the corporate performance management process.
- There is peer review of team member performance for high performing teams.
- Performance on teams is considered in all salary and promotion decisions.
- Recognition programs acknowledge team players in ways that demonstrate the importance of teamwork to the success of the organization.
- Team rewards are designed to encourage and foster collaborative behavior on the part of team members.
- Functional managers who support and encourage effective participation by their associates in cross-functional teams are valued and acknowledged.
- Teams find it easy to obtain resources that are necessary for their work, such as training in working virtually, information critical to their mission, and assistance in removing bureaucratic obstacles.

The Human Resources Challenge

Human resources professionals must incorporate the team player concept in all policies and procedures, creating a structure in which

- Recruitment literature and procedures make it clear that the organization values team players. In other words, soloists need not apply. The new team environment means that the hiring process needs to focus on experience in working collaboratively across functional departments, country boundaries, cultural differences, and telephone lines.

- Hiring interview questions and reference checks identify skills and experience in leading cross-functional, cross-cultural, and virtual teams.

- The performance appraisal process and competency studies used in salary plans are revised to include team player behaviors, cultural awareness, virtual team member effectiveness, and the ability to work with people from a variety of functional areas.

- Team player characteristics—including mastery of communications technologies, understanding the impact of cultural differences and the challenges of cross-functional collaboration, and knowledge and use of tools for developing trust and effective meeting facilitation—are added to the competencies in the organization's management assessment center.

The Learning and Development Challenge

Learning and development professionals must adapt their programs to help the organization make effective use of the new reality of global teamwork. At BT, a major employer in the UK, more than one-half of its 105,000 employees work in what are termed *remote teams*. To address this, says Caroline Waters, BT's director of people networks, their line manager training programs now teach a coaching and consultative style, because the old command-and-control approach just does not work with people who work remotely (Bell, 2003).

Learning and development professionals must offer workshops designed to help participants

- Develop effective team player skills
- Understand the elements of effective cross-functional teamwork
- Acquire the skills necessary to facilitate a successful meeting
- Cultivate a trusting and trust-building style
- Increase their competency in resolving conflicts in a team environment
- Sharpen skills in conducting an effective teleconference and video conference
- Widen their understanding of cultural differences and the impact of culture on effective teamwork
- Develop leadership skills needed to deal with the challenges of leading cross-functional, cross-cultural, and virtual teams

Workshops must also (1) provide managers with an awareness of the changing needs of teams in their organization and their role in supporting team-based efforts in their organization and (2) give senior managers an understanding of the importance of team rewards and team member recognition and tools to ensure successful programs in this area.

An additional learning and development challenge that comes from global teamwork is knowledge management and transfer. With people working in teams around the world, Shell International addressed the challenge of sharing expertise, lessons learned, and best practices by setting up "virtual communities of expertise" in which employees can bring problems and get answers (Bell, 2003). For example, an engineer in Louisiana might post a problem with a valve and get a response from another Shell engineer in Singapore who experienced the same problem the prior year and came up with a solution.

The Personal Challenge

For you, the challenge is to be the best possible team player. This means many things:

1. Know your style, including both your strengths and your potential for ineffectiveness.

2. Develop a plan to optimize your strengths and minimize your shortcomings.

3. Look for ways to expand your repertoire by increasing the use of the behaviors of other team player styles.

4. Be aware of your team's stage of development and the needs associated with that stage. Provide your team with the team player assistance required, and encourage others to do the same.

5. Acknowledge that other members of your team will have different styles. Be willing to work with others with different styles and to see this diversity as a team strength.

6. As a team leader, know the twelve dimensions of an effective team, assess your team's effectiveness, build on your strengths, and plan to reduce your weaknesses.

7. As a team leader, insist on team building for the team and team training for you and team members.

8. As a team leader, look for new and innovative ways to reward successes and recognize team members who go "above and beyond."

9. Persist and persevere. Teamwork is work.

10. And smile; you're having fun!

Resources

TOOLS FOR DEVELOPING TEAMS AND TEAM PLAYERS

A. Parker Team-Development Survey

B. Parker Team-Development Survey: Summary and Action Planning Guide

C. Parker Team Player Survey

D. Team Player Styles

E. Parker Team Player Survey: Normative Data Report

Note: The Parker Team-Development Survey and the Parker Team Player Survey may not be reproduced without express written permission from CPP, Inc. You may contact CPP, Inc. at 1055 Joaquin Road, 2nd Floor, Mountain View, CA 94043 or www.cpp.com.

Resource A

PARKER TEAM-DEVELOPMENT SURVEY

How often is this statement true?
(Circle one number)

Statements	Seldom		Sometimes		Often		Very Frequently	
1. *Clear Purpose:* The vision, mission, goal, or task of the team has been defined and is accepted by everyone. There is an action plan. Comments: _____	1	2	3	4	5	6	7	8
2. *Informality:* The climate tends to be informal, comfortable, and relaxed. There are no obvious tensions or signs of boredom. Comments: _____	1	2	3	4	5	6	7	8
3. *Participation:* There is a lot of discussion, and everyone is encouraged to participate. Comments: _____	1	2	3	4	5	6	7	8
4. *Listening:* The members use effective listening techniques such as questioning, paraphrasing, and summarizing to get out ideas. Comments: _____	1	2	3	4	5	6	7	8

Statements	Seldom		Sometimes		Often		Very Frequently	
5. *Civilized Disagreement:* There is disagreement, but the team is comfortable with this and shows no signs of avoiding, smoothing over, or suppressing conflict. Comments: _____	1	2	3	4	5	6	7	8
6. *Consensus Decisions:* For important decisions, the goal is substantial but not necessarily unanimous agreement through open discussion of everyone's ideas and avoidance of formal voting and easy compromises. Comments: _____	1	2	3	4	5	6	7	8
7. *Open Communication:* Team members feel free to express their feelings on the task as well as on the group's operation. There are few hidden agendas. Communication takes place outside of meetings. Comments: _____	1	2	3	4	5	6	7	8
8. *Clear Roles and Work Assignments:* There are clear expectations about the roles played by each team member. When action is taken, clear assignments are made, accepted, and carried out. Work is fairly distributed among team members. Comments: _____	1	2	3	4	5	6	7	8

Statements	Seldom		Sometimes		Often		Very Frequently	

9. *Shared Leadership*: Although the team has a formal leader, leadership functions shift from time to time depending on the circumstances, the needs of the group, and the skills of the members. The formal leader models the appropriate behavior and helps establish positive norms.
Comments: _____

           1 2 3 4 5 6 7 8

10. *External Relations*: The team spends time developing key outside relationships, mobilizing resources, and building credibility with important players in other parts of the organization.
Comments: _____

           1 2 3 4 5 6 7 8

11. *Style Diversity*: The team has a broad spectrum of team player types, including members who emphasize attention to tasks, goal setting, a focus on process, and questions about how the team is functioning.
Comments: _____

           1 2 3 4 5 6 7 8

12. *Self-Assessment*: Periodically, the team stops to examine how well it is functioning and what may be interfering with its effectiveness.
Comments: _____

           1 2 3 4 5 6 7 8

Resource B

PARKER TEAM-DEVELOPMENT SURVEY: SUMMARY AND ACTION PLANNING GUIDE

1. What are the strengths of your team?

2. In what areas do you need to improve?

3. Identify action steps to improve the functioning of your team.

Resource C

PARKER TEAM PLAYER SURVEY

Purpose

The *Parker Team Player Survey* will help you identify your style as a team player. The results will lead you to an assessment of your current strengths and provide a basis for a plan to increase your effectiveness as a team player.

Teams may use the survey to develop a profile of team strengths and to discuss strategies for increasing team effectiveness.

Directions

First, this is a survey, so there are no right or wrong answers. Please answer each item according to how you honestly feel you function now as a team member rather than how you used to be or how you would like to be.

You will be asked to complete eighteen sentences. Each sentence has four possible endings. Please rank the endings in the order in which you feel each one applies to you. Place the number 4 next to the ending that is most applicable to you and continue down to a 1 next to the ending that is least applicable to you.

For example:

As a team member, I am usually most concerned about

_____ a. meeting high ethical standards.

_____ b. reaching our goals.

_____ c. meeting my individual responsibilities.

_____ d. how well we are working together as a group.

Please do not make ties or use 4, 3, 2, or 1 more than once. It is possible that some of the sentences will have two or more endings that apply to you or will have none that applies to you, but you should assume these are your only choices and rank them accordingly. Each set of endings must be ranked with a 4, a 3, a 2, and a 1.

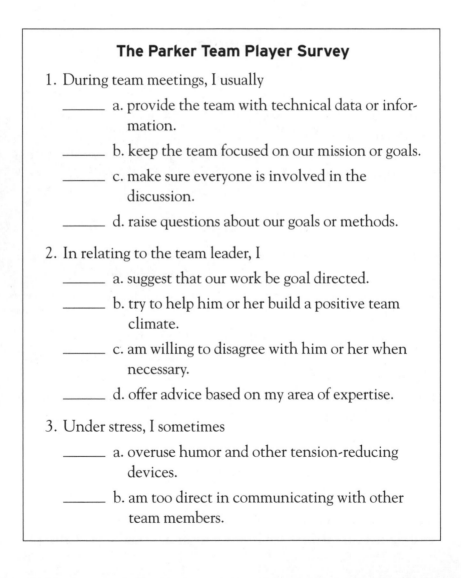

The Parker Team Player Survey

1. During team meetings, I usually

_____ a. provide the team with technical data or information.

_____ b. keep the team focused on our mission or goals.

_____ c. make sure everyone is involved in the discussion.

_____ d. raise questions about our goals or methods.

2. In relating to the team leader, I

_____ a. suggest that our work be goal directed.

_____ b. try to help him or her build a positive team climate.

_____ c. am willing to disagree with him or her when necessary.

_____ d. offer advice based on my area of expertise.

3. Under stress, I sometimes

_____ a. overuse humor and other tension-reducing devices.

_____ b. am too direct in communicating with other team members.

_____ c. lose patience with the need to get everyone involved in discussions.

_____ d. complain to outsiders about problems facing the team.

4. When conflicts arise on the team, I usually

_____ a. press for an honest discussion of the differences.

_____ b. provide reasons why one side or the other is correct.

_____ c. see the differences as a basis for a possible change in team direction.

_____ d. try to break the tension with a supportive or humorous remark.

5. Other team members usually see me as

_____ a. factual.

_____ b. flexible.

_____ c. encouraging.

_____ d. candid.

6. At times, I am

_____ a. too results oriented.

_____ b. too laid-back.

_____ c. self-righteous.

_____ d. shortsighted.

7. When things go wrong on the team, I usually

_____ a. push for increased emphasis on listening, feedback, and participation.

_____ b. press for candid discussion of our problems.

_____ c. work hard to provide more and better information.

_____ d. suggest that we revisit our basic mission.

8. A risky team contribution for me is to

_____ a. question some aspect of the team's work.

_____ b. push the team to set higher performance standards.

_____ c. work outside my defined role or job area.

_____ d. provide other team members with feedback on their behavior as team members.

9. Sometimes other team members see me as

_____ a. a perfectionist.

_____ b. unwilling to reassess the team's mission or goals.

_____ c. not serious about getting the real job done.

_____ d. a nitpicker.

10. I believe team problem solving requires

_____ a. cooperation by all team members.

_____ b. high-level listening skills.

_____ c. a willingness to ask tough questions.

_____ d. good solid data.

11. When a new team is forming, I usually

_____ a. try to meet and get to know other team members.

_____ b. ask pointed questions about our goals and methods.

_____ c. want to know what is expected of me.

_____ d. seek clarity about our basic mission.

12. At times, I make other people feel

_____ a. dishonest because they are not able to be as confrontational as I am.

_____ b. guilty because they don't live up to my standards.

_____ c. small-minded because they don't think long-range.

_____ d. heartless because they don't care about how people relate to each other.

13. I believe the role of the team leader is to

_____ a. ensure the efficient solution of business problems.

_____ b. help the team establish long-range goals and short-term objectives.

_____ c. create a participatory decision-making climate.

_____ d. bring out diverse ideas and challenge assumptions.

14. I believe team decisions should be based on

_____ a. the team's mission and goals.

_____ b. a consensus of team members.

_____ c. an open and candid assessment of the issues.

_____ d. the weight of the evidence.

15. Sometimes I

_____ a. see team climate as an end in itself.

_____ b. play devil's advocate far too long.

_____ c. fail to see the importance of effective team process.

_____ d. overemphasize strategic issues and minimize short-term task accomplishments.

16. People have often described me as

_____ a. independent.

_____ b. dependable.

_____ c. imaginative.

_____ d. participative.

17. Most of the time, I am

_____ a. responsible and hardworking.

_____ b. committed and flexible.

_____ c. enthusiastic and humorous.

_____ d. honest and authentic.

18. In relating to other team members, at times I get annoyed because they don't

_____ a. revisit team goals to check progress.

_____ b. see the importance of working well together.

_____ c. object to team actions with which they disagree.

_____ d. complete their team assignments on time.

Parker Team Player Survey Results

Directions

1. Please transfer your answers from the survey to this table.

2. Please be careful when recording the numbers in the following table, because the order of the letters differs from question to question. For example, for question #1 the order is a, b, c, d, but for question #2 the order is d, a, b, c.

3. The totals for the four styles must equal 180.

Question	Contributor	Collaborator	Communicator	Challenger
1.	a. ____	b. ____	c. ____	d. ____
2.	d. ____	a. ____	b. ____	c. ____
3.	c. ____	d. ____	a. ____	b. ____
4.	b. ____	c. ____	d. ____	a. ____
5.	a. ____	b. ____	c. ____	d. ____
6.	d. ____	a. ____	b. ____	c. ____
7.	c. ____	d. ____	a. ____	b. ____
8.	b. ____	c. ____	d. ____	a. ____
9.	a. ____	b. ____	c. ____	d. ____
10.	d. ____	a. ____	b. ____	c. ____
11.	c. ____	d. ____	a. ____	b. ____
12.	b. ____	c. ____	d. ____	a. ____
13.	a. ____	b. ____	c. ____	d. ____
14.	d. ____	a. ____	b. ____	c. ____
15.	b. ____	d. ____	a. ____	b. ____
16.	c. ____	c. ____	d. ____	a. ____
17.	a. ____	b. ____	c. ____	d. ____
18.	d. ____	a. ____	b. ____	c. ____
Totals	____	____	____	____ = 180

The highest number indicates your *primary team player style*. If your two highest numbers are the same or within three points of each other, consider them both as your primary style. The lowest total indicates your least-active team player style.

Your primary team player style defines a set of behaviors that you use most often as a member of a team. It does not mean that it is the only style you use. All of us have the capacity to use all of the four styles. We simply use one style—our primary style—most often.

Resource D

TEAM PLAYER STYLES

Contributor   *Task*

The Contributor is a task-oriented team member who enjoys providing the team with good technical information and data, does his or her homework, and pushes the team to set high performance standards and to use their resources wisely. Most people see you as dependable, although they believe that at times you may become too bogged down in the details and data or you fail to see the big picture or the need for a positive team climate.

People describe you as responsible, authoritative, reliable, proficient, and organized.

Collaborator   *Goal*

The Collaborator is a goal-directed member who sees the vision, mission, or goal of the team as paramount but is flexible and open to new ideas, willing to pitch in and work outside his or her defined role, and able to share the limelight with other team members. Most people see you as a big-picture person, but they believe that at times you may fail to revisit the mission periodically, give enough attention to the basic team tasks, or consider the individual needs of other team members.

People describe you as forward looking, goal directed, accommodating, flexible, and imaginative.

Communicator   *Process*

The Communicator is a process-oriented member who is an effective listener and facilitator of involvement, conflict resolution, consensus building, feedback, and the building of an informal, relaxed climate. Most people see you as a positive "people person," but they find that at times you may see process as an end in itself and that you may not confront other team members or give enough emphasis to completing task assignments and making progress toward team goals.

People describe you as supportive, considerate, relaxed, enthusiastic, and tactful.

Challenger   *Question*

The Challenger is a member who questions the goals, methods, and even the ethics of the team; is willing to disagree with the leader or higher authority; and encourages the team to take well-conceived risks. Most people appreciate the value of your candor and openness, but they think that at times you may not know when to back off an issue or you may become self-righteous and try to push the team too far.

People describe you as honest, outspoken, principled, ethical, and adventurous.

Resource E

PARKER TEAM PLAYER SURVEY: NORMATIVE DATA REPORT

Introduction

The *Parker Team Player Survey (PTPS)* is a self-report assessment of team player styles. The instrument originally appeared in the first edition of this book; as a result of initial analysis of the survey responses, several items have been modified.

In addition, a companion instrument has been developed: *Parker Team Player Survey: Styles of Another Person*. This instrument is completed by another team member so that the self-report can be compared with the perceptions of others on the team. Both surveys were published by Xicom, Incorporated in 1991. Xicom is now a subsidiary of CPP, Inc.

The *PTPS* yields four scores—one for each of the team player styles: Contributor, Collaborator, Communicator, and Challenger. The purpose of the *PTPS* is to increase awareness of the behaviors required for effective teamwork. In a training workshop it is used as a diagnostic tool to help participants identify and understand their strengths and potential weaknesses as a team player. Further, they use the results to shape an action plan to increase their effectiveness as a team player by building on their strengths, expanding their repertoire, reducing their ineffective behaviors, and improving their communication with other team players.

Note: For more ideas on how to use the PTPS in training and team building, see G. M. Parker, *Parker Team Building Program: Facilitator's Guide* (Mountain View, Calif.: CPP, Inc., 2003, www.cpp.com).

In a team building session with an intact team, the *PTPS* results are used to improve personal effectiveness (especially if the self-report is combined with the *Styles of Another Person* surveys completed by other team members) and interpersonal communication among team members and to increase overall team effectiveness by analyzing the style distribution on the team. The *PTPS* can be used in similar ways in an inter-group team building session.

It is important to understand that a person has the capacity to use the strengths of any of the four styles. Most people (about 65 percent) use one style more often than others. A person can be an effective team player using just one of the four styles, provided the person optimizes her or his strengths and minimizes weaknesses. However, the most effective team player, regardless of primary style, is able to use the strengths of any of the styles as required by the team. Similarly, an effective team is one in which all four styles are used as required by the situation.

Data Collection

The data for this norms report were collected during a seven-year period from 1989 to 2000. All of the data reported are from *Parker Team Player Surveys* completed during training workshops, team building sessions, and team meetings. Participants were from a wide variety of industries and occupations. Although most of the people in the sample work for private sector organizations, some are employed by government and nonprofit agencies.

In all, about 3,400 people are included in this sample. Data collection is ongoing; updates of this report will be made available on www.glennparker.com. Sample sizes vary from table to table because the same demographic data were not collected at each administration of the *PTPS*.

Overall Style Distribution (Table E.1)

Among the approximately 3,400 people who completed the *PTPS*, 65 percent had one primary style, 29 percent had two primary styles, 5 percent had three styles, and less than 1 percent had a uniform distribution. These data indicate that the *PTPS* does yield a single primary style for about seven out of ten people who complete the survey.

Among all people who completed the *PTPS*, the most frequently reported styles were Collaborator, with 24 percent of the total, and Contributor, with 18 percent. The Challenger, with about 12 percent, and the Communicator, with 10 percent, were the least frequent. Of the 2,191 people with a single primary style, Contributors and Collaborators accounted for 61 percent.

It is also interesting to note that among the people with two primary styles, the Contributor-Collaborator combination accounted for almost a third of the total in this category. Therefore, looking at overall style distribution, it is fair to conclude that the Contributor and Collaborator styles appear most frequently in the total group studied.

Style Distribution by Gender (Table E.2)

Among both men and women in the sample, Collaborator is the most frequently reported style with about 22 percent. The similarities between men and women end at that point. The second most frequently reported style among men is Contributor, with 18 percent, while the second highest among women is Challenger, with 18 percent.

The most dramatic differences occur when the Challenger results are compared. About 18 percent of the women in the sample are Challengers whereas 12 percent of the men are Challengers. Among people with a single primary style, one quarter (26 percent) of the women are Challengers, making it the second highest category among women. However, Challengers account for only 18 percent of the men, making it the second lowest style among men.

Style Distribution by Occupation (Table E.3)

Among professionals, the most frequently reported styles are Contributor (18.2 percent) and Collaborator (20 percent). Only 13 percent of the professionals in the sample are Challengers and 11 percent are Communicators.

The results for executives and managers are quite similar. The most frequently reported style for both is Collaborator, with 26 percent and 25 percent, respectively. In contrast with the professionals category, 21 percent of the executives and 17 percent of the managers are Challengers, making it the second largest category for both.

Looking at the wage earners in the group studied, we find Collaborator (23 percent) as the most frequently reported style followed by Contributor (18 percent). The percentage of Communicators is quite low (8 percent); however, the sample size is small.

Style Distribution by Industry (Table E.4)

The financial services industry data are interesting because the Communicator (23.3 percent) is right up there with the Collaborator (24.3 percent) as the most frequently reported styles.

Although the sample size is small, the chemical industry shows a high percentage of Contributors (18 percent) and Collaborators (18 percent) as well as the Contributor-Collaborator combination (18 percent). Challengers and Communicators each account for only 9 percent of the total.

The pharmaceutical industry results are quite dramatic. A large percentage (23 percent) of the sample are Contributors, whereas only 12 percent are Challengers and 5 percent are Communicators.

In telecommunications the most frequent styles are Contributor (22 percent) and Collaborator (21 percent) as well as the Contributor-Collaborator two-style combination (10 percent). Only 6 percent are Communicators and 12 percent are Challengers.

Almost one-quarter (24 percent) of government employees are Collaborators; the results among the other three styles are remarkably similar: Contributor (14 percent), Communicator (14 percent), Challenger (12 percent).

The health care results are quite interesting. The most frequent style is Collaborator, with 28 percent, but the next most frequent style is Challenger, with more than 20 percent of the sample.

In the manufacturing sector, there is a fairly even distribution among the four styles: Contributor tops the list with 18 percent, followed by Collaborator at 17 percent, Communicator at 16 percent, and Challenger at 15 percent.

Table E.1 Parker Team Player Survey: Distribution by Number of Primary Styles

Team Player Style	Subgroup N	Subgroup %	Total N	Total %
One Primary Style			2,191	65%
Contributor	626	18.4		
Collaborator	820	24.1		
Communicator	347	10.2		
Challenger	398	11.7		
Two Primary Styles			987	29%
Contributor-Collaborator	307	9.1		
Contributor-Communicator	68	2.4		
Contributor-Challenger	171	5.0		
Collaborator-Communicator	174	5.2		
Collaborator-Challenger	164	4.8		
Communicator-Challenger	103	2.8		
Three Primary Styles			177	5.2%
Contributor-Collaborator-Communicator	43	1.3		
Contributor-Collaborator-Challenger	68	2.0		
Contributor-Communicator-Challenger	34	1.0		
Collaborator-Communicator-Challenger	36	1.1		
Four Styles			31	0.8%

N = 3,386

Table E.2 Parker Team Player Survey: Style Distribution by Gender

Team Player Style	Men N	Men %	Women N	Women %	Total N	Total %
One Primary Style						
Contributor	239	18.2	176	11.7	415	14.8
Collaborator	291	22.4	321	21.5	612	21.8
Communicator	129	9.8	191	12.8	320	11.4
Challenger	141	10.7	275	18.4	416	14.8
Two Primary Styles						
Contributor-Collaborator	117	9.0	154	10.3	271	9.7
Contributor-Communicator	22	1.6	46	3.0	68	2.4
Contributor-Challenger	92	7.0	62	4.1	154	5.9
Collaborator-Communicator	76	5.8	92	6.0	168	6.0
Collaborator-Challenger	86	6.5	57	3.7	143	5.1
Communicator-Challenger	47	3.6	51	3.3	98	3.4
Three Primary Styles						
Contributor-Collaborator-Communicator	27	2.1	14	0.9	41	1.5
Contributor- Collaborator-Challenger	22	1.7	23	1.5	45	1.6
Contributor-Communicator-Challenger	6	0.5	14	0.9	20	0.7
Collaborator-Communicator-Challenger	9	0.7	9	0.5	18	0.6
Four Styles	8	0.6	11	0.7	19	0.6
N = 2,808	**1,312**		**1,496**		**2,808**	

Table E.3 Parker Team Player Survey: Style Distribution by Occupation

Team Player Style	Executives N	Executives %	Managers N	Managers %	Professionals N	Professionals %	Wage N	Wage %	Total N	Total %
One Primary Style										
Contributor	15	15.8	62	13.5	181	18.2	30	17.6	288	16.7
Collaborator	26	27.3	117	25.4	199	20.0	39	22.9	381	22.1
Communicator	10	10.5	55	12.0	117	11.7	14	8.2	196	11.4
Challenger	21	22.1	80	17.4	129	13.0	19	11.2	249	14.5
Two Primary Styles										
Contributor-Collaborator	9	9.5	28	6.1	104	10.4	22	12.9	163	9.5
Contributor-Communicator	1	1.1	9	2.0	27	2.7	2	1.2	39	2.3
Contributor-Challenger	1	1.1	24	5.2	52	5.2	9	5.3	86	5.0
Collaborator-Communicator	2	2.1	30	6.5	54	5.4	6	3.5	92	5.5
Collaborator-Challenger	5	5.3	22	4.8	49	4.9	8	4.7	84	4.9
Communicator-Challenger	1	1.1	12	2.6	31	3.1	6	3.5	50	2.9
Three Primary Styles										
Contributor-Collaborator-Communicator	1	1.1	3	0.7	15	1.5	4	2.4	23	1.3
Contributor-Collaborator-Challenger	0	0.0	9	2.0	10	1.0	3	1.8	22	1.2
Contributor-Communicator-Challenger	1	1.1	5	1.1	8	0.8	4	2.4	18	1.1
Collaborator-Communicator-Challenger	2	2.1	1	0.2	12	1.2	2	1.2	17	1.0
Four Styles	0	0.0	3	0.7	8	0.8	2	1.2	13	0.8
N = 1,721	95		460		996		170		1,721	

Table E.4 Parker Team Player Survey: Style Distribution by Industry

Team Player Style	Finan. N	Finan. %	Chem. N	Chem. %	Pharma. N	Pharma. %	Telecom. N	Telecom. %	Gov't. N	Gov't. %	Health N	Health %	Manufact. N	Manufact. %	Total N	Total %
One Primary Style																
Contributor	25	13.0	16	17.8	108	23.0	36	21.8	27	13.6	21	12.9	46	18.0	279	19.4
Collaborator	47	24.3	16	17.8	97	20.7	35	21.2	48	24.1	45	27.6	42	16.5	330	21.5
Communicator	45	23.3	8	8.9	25	5.3	10	6.1	28	14.1	20	12.1	40	15.7	176	12.7
Challenger	28	14.5	8	8.9	56	12.0	20	12.1	24	12.1	33	20.2	39	15.3	208	12.1
Two Primary Styles																
Contributor-Collaborator	15	7.8	16	17.8	56	12.0	17	10.3	19	9.6	10	6.1	24	9.4	157	10.7
Contributor-Communicator	3	1.6	2	2.2	13	2.8	6	3.6	2	1.0	2	1.2	4	1.6	32	2.3
Contributor-Challenger	5	2.6	5	5.6	31	6.6	12	7.3	13	6.5	6	3.7	9	3.5	81	5.0
Collaborator-Communicator	6	3.1	3	3.3	16	3.4	8	4.8	21	10.6	7	4.3	20	7.8	81	4.9
Collaborator-Challenger	6	3.1	4	4.4	27	5.8	8	4.8	6	3.0	8	4.9	14	5.5	73	4.1
Communicator-Challenger	4	2.1	3	3.3	9	1.9	6	3.6	3	1.5	4	2.5	4	1.6	33	2.0
Three Primary Styles																
Contributor-Collaborator-Communicator	2	1.0	2	2.2	7	1.5	2	1.2	1	0.5	2	1.2	2	0.8	18	1.3
Contributor-Collaborator-Challenger	3	1.6	1	1.1	10	2.1	2	1.2	3	1.5	2	1.2	6	2.4	27	1.7
Contributor-Communicator-Challenger	0	0.0	4	4.4	5	1.1	0	0.0	1	0.5	1	0.6	1	0.4	12	0.8
Collaborator-Communicator-Challenger	2	1.0	1	1.1	3	0.6	3	1.8	~2	1.0	1	0.6	3	1.2	15	0.9
Four Styles	2	1.0	1	1.1	5	1.1	0	0.0	1	0.5	1	0.6	1	1.2	11	0.5
N = 1,533	193		90		468		165		199		163		255		1,533	

References

Anawati, D., and Craig, A. "Behavioral Adaptation Within Cross-Cultural Virtual Teams." *IEEE Transactions on Professional Communication*, March 2006, pp. 44–56.

Ancona, D. G., and Caldwell, D. *Speeding Product Development: Making Teamwork Work.* Cambridge, Mass.: Sloan School of Management, 1992.

Andres, H. P. "A Comparison of Face-to-Face and Virtual Software Development Teams." *Team Performance Management*, 2002, 8(1/2), 39–48.

Argyris, C. *Integrating the Individual and the Organization.* Hoboken, N.J.: Wiley, 1964.

Asherman, I. "Language, Culture and the Drug Development Process." *DIA Today*, 2005, 5(3), 28.

Atkins, S. *The Name of Your Game.* Beverly Hills, Calif.: Ellis & Stewart, 1981.

Baba, M., Gluesing, J., Ratner, H., and Wagner, K. "The Context of Knowing: Natural History of a Globally Distributed Team." *Journal of Organizational Behavior*, 2004, 25, 547–587.

Barczak, G., McDonough, E. F., and Athanassiou, N. "So You Want to Be a Global Project Leader?" *Research-Technology Management*, May/June 2006, pp. 28–35.

Barmore, G. T. "Teamwork: Charting a Course for Success." *Mortgage Banking*, Aug. 1987, pp. 92–96.

Bell, S. "Remote Control." *Human Resources*, Sept. 2003, pp. 44–46.

Bennis, W. G. Speech presented at Best of America Human Resources Conference sponsored by *Training Magazine* and *Personnel Journal*, New York, Dec. 12, 1988.

Bennis, W. G. *Why Leaders Can't Lead: The Unconscious Conspiracy Continues.* San Francisco: Jossey-Bass, 1989.

Bennis, W. G., and Nanus, B. *Leaders: The Strategies for Taking Charge.* New York: Harper & Row, 1985.

Note: Some references listed here are not cited in the text but were helpful in shaping my thinking.

Beranek, P. M., and Martz, B. "Making Virtual Teams More Effective: Improving Relational Links." *Team Performance Management*, 2005, *11*(5/6), 200–213.

Blake, R., and Mouton, J. S. *The Managerial Grid*. Houston, Tex.: Gulf, 1964.

Block, P. *The Empowered Manager: Positive Political Skills at Work*. San Francisco: Jossey-Bass, 1987.

Bradford, D., and Cohen, A. R. *Managing for Excellence*. Hoboken, N.J.: Wiley, 1984.

Briggs, K. C., and Myers, I. B. *Myers-Briggs Type Indicator (F)*. Princeton, N.J.: Educational Testing Service, 1957.

Cespedes, F. V., Doyle, S. X., and Freedman, R. J. "Teamwork for Today's Selling." *Harvard Business Review*, Mar.-Apr. 1989, pp. 44–48.

Chance, P. "Great Experiments in Team Chemistry."*Across the Board*, May 1989, pp. 18–24.

Chubb, J. E. "Why the Current Wave of School Reform Will Fail." *The Public Interest*, Winter 1988, pp. 28–49.

Cohen, S. S. "Beyond Macho: The Power of Womanly Management." *Working Woman*, Feb. 1989, pp. 77–83.

Conger, J., and Lawler, E. "People Skills Still Rule in a Virtual Company." *Financial Times*, Aug. 26, 2005, p. 10.

"Copy Cats Worth Copying." *Management Solutions*, Jan. 1988, p. 28.

Crosby, P. *Quality Is Free*. New York: New American Library, 1979.

Dayal, I., and Thomas, J. M. "Operation KPE: Developing a New Organization." *Journal of Applied Behavioral Science*, 1968, 4(4), 473–506.

Deal, T. E., and Kennedy, A. A. *Corporate Culture*. Reading, Mass: Addison-Wesley, 1982.

Dionne, J. L. "The Art of Acquisitions." *Journal of Business Strategy*, Nov.-Dec. 1988, 9, pp. 12–18.

Drexler, A. B., Sibbet, D., and Forrester, R. H. "The Team Performance Model." In W. B. Reddy and K. Lamison (eds.), *Team Building*. Alexandria, Va.: NTL Institute for Applied Behavior Science, 1988.

Dudlicek, J. "Team Players." *Dairy Field*, Apr. 2003, pp. 28–33.

Dyer, W. G. *Team Building: Issues and Alternatives*. Reading, Mass.: Addison-Wesley, 1987.

"Ethical Values and Principles." *Ethics: Easier Said Than Done*, Spring/Summer 1988, p. 153.

Feder, R., and Mitchell, J. "4-day Task Force More Efficient Than Traditional Problem-Solving." *Marketing News*, Aug. 29, 1988, p. 21.

Franke, J. J., Jr. "Innovation and Teamwork." *The Bureaucrat*, Winter 1988–89, pp. 11–12.

Gedvilas, C. "Recognizing and Rewarding Team Performance at Motorola." *ACA News*, Feb. 1997, 40(2), 6–9.

George, B., and Sims, P. *True North: Discover Your Authentic Leadership*. San Francisco: Jossey-Bass, 2007.

Gordon, J. "Do Virtual Teams Deliver Only Virtual Performance?" *Training*, June 2005, pp. 20–25.

Gross, S., and Blair, J. "Reinforcing Team Effectiveness Through Pay." *Compensation and Benefits Review*, Sept.-Oct. 1995, pp. 34–38.

Hackman, J. R. *Leading Teams: Setting the Stage for Great Performances*. Boston: Harvard Business School Press, 2002.

Harrison, R. "Role Negotiations." In W. Burke and H. Hornstein (eds.), *The Social Technology of Organization Development*. Washington, D.C.: NTL Learning Resources, 1971.

Hart, L. B. *Learning from Conflict*. Reading, Mass.: Addison-Wesley, 1980.

Harvey, J. "The Abilene Paradox: The Management of Agreement." *Organizational Dynamics*, Summer 1974, pp. 17–34.

Hastings, C., Bixby, P., and Chaudhry-Lawton, R. *The Superteam Solution*. San Diego, Calif.: University Associates, 1987.

Herman, S. M., and Herman, M. D. "Special Teams, Properly Used, Can Create Effective Solutions." *Personnel Administrator*, Oct. 1989, pp. 90–92.

Hong, P., Nahm, A. Y., and Doll, W. J. "The Role of Project Target Clarity in an Uncertain Project Environment." *International Journal of Operations and Production Management*, 2004, 24(12), 1269–1291.

Hughes, L. "How to Be an Effective Team Player." *Women in Business*, Nov.-Dec. 2003, p. 22.

Isen, A. M., Daubman, K. A., and Nowicki, G. P. "Positive Affect Facilitates Creative Problem Solving." *Journal of Personality and Social Psychology*, June 1987, pp. 1122–1131.

Jackall, R. "Moral Mazes: Bureaucracy and Managerial Work." *Harvard Business Review*, Sept.-Oct. 1983, pp. 118–130.

Jamieson, D. "Aligning the Organization for a Team-based Strategy." In G. Parker (ed.), *Handbook of Best Practices for Teams*, Vol. 1, pp. 299–312. Amherst, Mass.: HRD Press, 1996.

Janus, I. *Victims of Groupthink*. Boston: Houghton Mifflin, 1972.

Jarvenpaa, S. L., Shaw, T. R., and Staples, D. S. "Toward Contextual Theories of Trust: The Role of Trust in Global Virtual Teams." *Information Systems Research*, Sept. 2004, pp. 250–267.

Johnson, D. "There Is No 'I' in Team." *American Printer*, Aug. 2000, pp. 44–47.

Jung, C. G. *Psychological Types*. New York: Pantheon Books, 1923.

Kador, J. "Leveraging Process Improvement." *InfoWorld*, Mar. 19, 2001, pp. 39–40.

Kahane, E. "Trust and Powerful Learning." *Training and Development*, July 2006, pp. 51–54.

Kanter, R. M. *The Change Masters*. New York: Simon & Schuster, 1983.

Kapstein, J., and Hoerr, J. "Volvo's Radical New Plant: The Death of the Assembly Line?" *Business Week*, Aug. 28, 1989, pp. 92–93.

Katzenbach, J. R., and Smith, D. K. *The Wisdom of Teams: Creating the High Performance Organization*. Boston: Harvard Business School Press, 1993.

Kertesz, L. "Team Concept Makes Mazda Flat Rock a Different Plant." *Automotive News*, Feb. 29, 1988, p. 36.

Klein, S. *The Science of Happiness*. New York: Marlowe, 2002.

Kohn, A. *No Contest*. Boston: Houghton Mifflin, 1986.

Kohn, A. *Punished by Rewards: The Trouble with Gold Stars, Incentive Plans, A's, Praise, and Other Bribes*. New York: Houghton Mifflin, 1993.

Kouzes, J. M., and Posner, B. Z. *The Leadership Challenge: How to Get Extraordinary Things Done in Organizations*. San Francisco: Jossey-Bass, 1987.

Lambert, L. "The End of the Era of Staff Development." *Educational Leadership*, 1989, 7(1), 79–81.

Larson, C. E., and LaFasto, F.M.J. *Teamwork: What Must Go Right/What Can Go Wrong*. Thousand Oaks, Calif.: Sage, 1989.

Lawler, E. E., III. *High-Involvement Management: Participative Strategies for Improving Organizational Performance*. San Francisco: Jossey-Bass, 1986.

Lee, B. "Worker Harmony Makes NUMMI Work." *New York Times*, Dec. 25, 1988, Sec. 3, p. 2.

Lewin, K. *Field Theory in Social Science*. New York: Harper & Row, 1951.

Likert, R. *New Patterns of Management*. New York: McGraw-Hill, 1961.

McAdams, J. *The Reward Plan Advantage*. San Francisco: Jossey-Bass, 1996.

McGee, E. C. "Peer Evaluation: Coaching for Coaching." In G. Parker (ed.), *Handbook of Best Practices for Teams*, Vol. 2, pp. 311–326. Amherst, Mass.: HRD Press, 1998.

McGregor, D. M. *The Human Side of Enterprise*. New York: McGraw-Hill, 1960.

Metrex Footnotes. Newsletter. Tryon, N.C.: Mnetrex, Dec. 1988.

Miles, S. J., and Mangold, G. "The Impact of Team Leader Performance on Team Member Satisfaction: The Subordinate's Perspective." *Team Performance Journal*, 2002, 8(5/6), 113–121.

Mower, J. G., and Wilemon, D. "Rewarding Technical Teamwork." *Research-Technology Management*, Sept.-Oct. 1989, pp. 24–29.

Myerson, D., Weick, D. E., and Kramer, R. M. "Swift Trust and Temporary Groups." In R. M. Kramer and T. R. Tyler (eds.), *Trust in Organizations: Frontiers of Theory and Research*, pp. 166–195. Thousand Oaks, Calif.: Sage, 1996.

Oertig, M., and Buergi, T. "The Challenges of Managing Cross-Cultural Virtual Teams." *Team Performance Management*, 2006, 12(1/2), 23–30.

Parker, G. *Team Depot: A Warehouse of Over 585 Tools to Reassess, Rejuvenate, and Rehabilitate Your Team*. San Francisco: Pfeiffer, 2002.

Parker, G. *Cross-Functional Teams: Working with Allies, Enemies, and Other Strangers*. San Francisco: Jossey-Bass, 2003.

Parker, G., and Hoffman, R. *Meeting Excellence: Tools to Lead Meetings That Get Results*. San Francisco: Jossey-Bass, 2006.

Parker, G., McAdams, J., and Zielinski, D. *Rewarding Teams: Lessons from the Trenches*. San Francisco: Jossey-Bass, 2003.

Peters, T. *Thriving on Chaos.* New York: Knopf, 1987.

Pugh, D. S., and Hickson, D. J. *Writers on Organizations.* Thousand Oaks, Calif.: Sage, 1989.

Reeves, R. "Enough of the T-Word." *Management Today,* Mar. 2004, p. 29.

Robbins, H., and Finley, M. *Why Teams Don't Work.* Lawrenceville, N.J.: Peterson's, 1995.

Rosenberg, M. "60 Minutes You'll Never Get Back." *Training and Development,* Mar. 2006, p. 14.

Rowe, A. J., and Mason, R. O. *Managing with Style: A Guide to Understanding, Assessing, and Improving Decision Making.* San Francisco: Jossey-Bass, 1987.

Rowh, M. "How to Be a Team Player." *Career World,* Oct. 2001, p. 25.

Schultz-Hardt, S., and others. "Group Decision-Making in Hidden Profile Situations: Dissent as a Facilitator for Decision Quality." *Journal of Personality and Social Psychology,* Dec. 2006, 1080–1093.

Straub, J. T. "Dealing with the Talented Loner on the Team." *Getting Results . . . for the Hands-on Manager,* 1997, 42(7), 8.

Taninecz, G. "Team Players." *Industry Week,* July 15, 1996, pp. 28–33.

Traub, J. "Into the Mouths of Babes." *New York Times Magazine,* July 24, 1988, pp. 18–53.

Tuckman, B. W. "Developmental Sequence in Small Groups." *Psychological Bulletin,* 1965, 63(6), 384–399.

Walton, R. *Interpersonal Peacemaking: Confrontation and Third Party Consultation.* Reading, Mass.: Addison-Wesley, 1969.

Wilson, J. M., George, J., Wellins, R. S., and Byham, W. *Leadership Trapeze: Strategies for Leadership in Team-Based Organizations,* San Francisco: Jossey-Bass, 1994.

Yu, L. "How Team Communication Affects Innovation." *MIT Sloan Management Review,* Summer 2005, p. 8.

Zenger, J. H., Musselwhite, E., Horson, K., and Perrin, C. *Leading Teams: Mastering the New Role.* Burr Ridge, Ill.: Irwin Professional Publishing, 1994.

Zigon, J. *How to Measure Team Performance.* Wallingford, Penn.: Zigon Performance Group, 1999.

Index

H

H-E-B Grocery, 123, 169
Hackman, J. R., 115, 118
Harrison, R., 49
Hart, L. B., 38
Harvey, J., 156
Hastings, C., 55, 58
Hawthorne project, 14
Henrick, T. "Old Reliable," 76
Hoerr, J., 4
Hoffman, R., 23, 81
Honesty, 95
Horson, K., 115
Human resources challenge, 186
The Human Side of Enterprise (McGregor),
    15
Humor, 87

I

IBM, 21
Ineffective team leaders
    Challenger as, 125–126
    Collaborator as, 121–122
    Communicator as, 123–124
    Contributor as, 119
Ineffective team players
    assessing yourself as possible, 102e
    Challenger as, 109–110
    Collaborator as, 105–107
    Communicator as, 107–108
    confronting, 113–114
    contacting the boss of, 113
    Contributor as, 104–105
    cost of, 103–104
    dealing with other team members
        as, 111–114
    dealing with yourself as, 110–111
    overview of issues connected
        to, 101–102
    transferring, reassigning, or firing, 114
    See also Conflict
Ineffective teams
    description of, 63–64
    warning signs of, 64–67
Informal climate, 24–26
Information system, 169
Innovativeness, 170, 171
Institute for Social Research (University
    of Michigan), 16
"Invisible team members," 55–58
Isen, A. M., 25

J

Jackall, R., 92
Jamieson culture model
    culture element of, 180–181
    described, 163
    rewards and recognition element
        of, 175–180
    strategy element of, 164–166
    structure element of, 166–168
    systems element of, 168–174
Jamieson, D., 6, 163, 173
Janus, I., 141, 156
Job centered managers, 16
Johnson & Johnson, 74, 79, 88, 161
Jones, J., 18
Jung, C., 70

K

Kador, J., 175
Kahane, E., 46, 47
Kanter, R. M., 1
Kapstein, J., 4
Katzenbach, J. R., 5, 18, 21
Keithley Instruments, 3
Kennedy, A. A., 180
Kertesz, L., 4
Klein, S., 23
Kohn, A., 183
Kouzes, J. M., 115
Kramer, R. M., 47

L

LaFasto, F.M.J., 5, 22
Lambert, L., 3
Larson, C. E., 5, 22
Lawler, E. E., III, 1, 56
Leadership
    changing view of, 115
    definition of, 53
    shared, 52–54
    task and process responsibilities
        of, 53, 55t
    See also Managers; Team leaders
Learning
    challenges regarding development
        and, 186–187
    organizational culture regarding
        development and, 174
    workshops offered to facilitate, 187
Lee, B., 4